CENTRAL LENDING RENEWALS 273-4729

- 5 JAN 2010
25 1,

1 7 MAY 2010

1 9 MAY 2011
28·10·19

L63   **Sheffield** CL   R55
City Council

Please return/renew this item
by the last date shown.

Items may also be renewed by
phone and Internet.

LIBRARIES, ARCHIVES & INFORMATION

D0522151

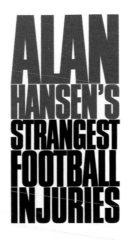

ALAN HANSEN'S STRANGEST FOOTBALL INJURIES

Sport Media

Cover design: Jamie Dunmore
Design and proofing: James Cleary, Glen Hind and Lee Ashun

Produced by Sport Media, Trinity Mirror North West

Executive Editor: Ken Rogers. Senior Editor: Steve Hanrahan
Senior Production Editor: Paul Dove.
Senior Art Editor: Rick Cooke
Sub Editors: Roy Gilfoyle, James Cleary,
Michael Haydock, Adam Oldfield
Designers: Glen Hind, Colin Sumpter, Barry Parker, Lee Ashun,
Alison Gilliland, Jamie Dunmore, James Kenyon, Lisa Critchley
Writers: Chris McLoughlin, David Randles,
Gavin Kirk, John Hynes, Simon Hughes,
William Hughes, Alan Jewell
Sales and Marketing Manager: Elizabeth Morgan
Sales and marketing assistant: Karen Cadman

Published in Great Britain in 2009 by:
Trinity Mirror Sport Media,
PO Box 48, Old Hall Street, Liverpool L69 3EB.

All Rights Reserved. No part of this publication may be
reproduced, stored in a retrieval system, or transmitted in any form,
or by any means, electronic, mechanical, photocopying, recording
or otherwise without the prior permission in writing of the copyright
holders, nor be otherwise circulated in any form of binding or cover
other than in which it is published and without a similar condition
being imposed on the subsequent publisher.

ISBN: 9781906802387

Photographs: PA Photos

Printed by Korotan

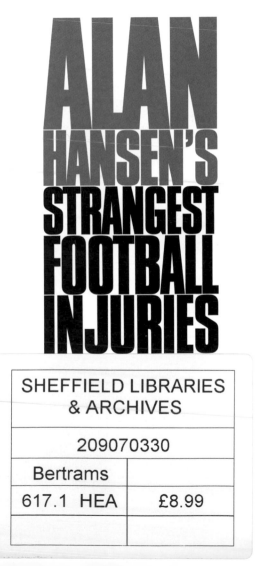

ALAN HANSEN'S STRANGEST FOOTBALL INJURIES

SHEFFIELD LIBRARIES & ARCHIVES	
209070330	
Bertrams	
617.1 HEA	£8.99

CONTENTS

INJURIES HAVE ALWAYS PLAYED A BIG PART IN FOOTBALL

FOLLOWING a playing career that lasted 18 years and nearly two decades of punditry since on Match of the Day, I have witnessed and grimaced and laughed at many football injuries. They are part and parcel of the game but nothing can prepare you for when they happen. I sympathise with any footballer that suffers a serious injury because a treatment room at any club is a lonely place. But as you will see in this book, there have been many injuries sustained in strange circumstances.

Some players can be remembered throughout their whole career and long after they have retired for the way they sustained a peculiar injury. Injuries have always played a big part in football. They can be the difference between success and failure. For me, it provided an opportunity.

If it wasn't for an injury to Tommy Smith, I might not have got my chance in the 1978 European Cup final

Tommy accidentally injured his foot with a pick-axe in the weeks leading up to the match against Club Brugge at Wembley. I'd only been a sub in the games towards the end of the season, and wasn't expecting too many minutes on the pitch as the final approached.

When I was told that I would be in the team in the penultimate league fixture against West Ham, I was surprised because I didn't have any inkling at all that Tommy was injured.

I managed to retain my place in the following weeks then started against Brugge. My career really took off from there.

Tommy was a player associated with ferocious tackling. But he was a fine footballer too. One of the nastiest challenges I ever witnessed was between Tommy and Larry Lloyd in the League Cup final at Wembley. There may have been a bit of history between them from their time together at Liverpool.

The ball was in the centre circle and both players ran 15 yards either side to try and win possession. Nobody got near it. The studs were showing and it was a terrible tangle. Thankfully, they both got up and walked away. It was my first season at Liverpool and I was thinking, 'what the hell have I let myself in for here?'

Tommy was a fierce competitor and the problems later in life with his knees have been well documented. None of his injuries, though, were really a result of his tenacity on the pitch. It was because of the way he tackled by leading with one leg and sliding with the other on his knee, coupled with the cortisones he took to get through so many games. Like quite a few players from his time, and like me, he played in many games that he shouldn't have and he's paying the price now.

The risk of injury in football is commonplace, but the big thing that has changed since the days when I played is the approach to rehabilitation.

Between 1962 and 1986, Liverpool didn't change any of the machinery or technology related to player recovery. You might say that was a failing, but they will say and be able to prove that it wasn't a failing because few players at the club suffered really serious injuries and we achieved so much success.

If you were injured, you were persona non grata. You'd be ignored totally and the only question the management would ask you was: 'When are you going to be fit?'

For some footballers, the approach to recovering from injuries was a mental barrier. If one of the management asked a player whether they were going to be fit for Saturday and the

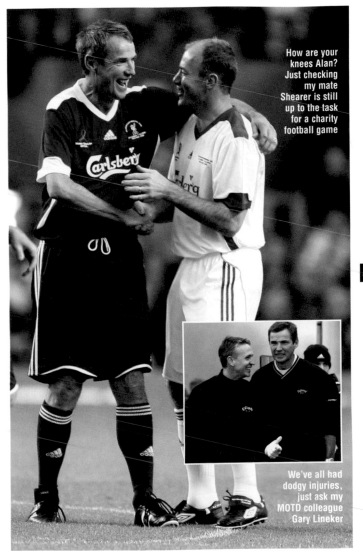

How are your knees Alan? Just checking my mate Shearer is still up to the task for a charity football game

We've all had dodgy injuries, just ask my MOTD colleague Gary Lineker

Bob Paisley:
Another one for
the ultrasound
machine at
Anfield

player said it was going to be touch and go, you knew he wasn't going to play. But as a player, if you got the cold shoulder, it made you want to play more because there's nothing worse than being on the sidelines away from all your team-mates.

The basic treatment was ultrasound. Whether you had a bad hamstring, groin, thigh, knee, broken leg or flu, that's what they gave you for five minutes a day across the best part of a week. If that didn't work and you didn't play on a Saturday, you'd be sent to a specialist and they'd jab you with cortisone – which later on, we found was totally wrong.

When they finally came to replace the ultrasound machine under Kenny Dalglish in the mid-80s, the guy who came and looked at it said that it wasn't a machine that was appropriate for using on humans. Apparently it was better for deep muscle injuries on animals like horses. They said we were thoroughbreds, but using an ultrasound that was meant for horses was a bit extreme.

There was another method if you were particularly bad where they got three pads and wired it up. It was like an electric shock treatment and it was turned on and off manually. We had an Irish doctor and whenever he went into the room to see if the player was responding to the treatment, he'd accidentally flick the switch with his knee and give the player an almighty shock. It was quite a comical scene if you think about it, but it didn't half hurt. It was torture, but after a few sessions on that, none of the players wanted to see the treatment room for a long time, so they remained 'fit.' The idea was to make you feel as low as you possibly could, so you would play.

There's a great story about Jimmy Melia where Shanks forgot to turn the machine on. So Jimmy kept telling Shanks to switch the settings higher and higher, but nothing was happening. All of a sudden, Shanks realised there was an 'on' switch so he pressed it. Jimmy nearly hit the roof. Shanks said: "I've never seen you jump so high Jimmy."

Liverpool Football Club was the best at everything on the

pitch for three decades, but their approach to treatment of injured players was quite farcical, with hindsight. Then again, when Kenny brought all the modern technology in so the club's medical staff could deal with injuries properly, all of a sudden, we never had so many injuries.

People today say that there are more games in a season if your club are competing for major honours – which is true. But clubs have bigger squads now to deal with such obstacles as fatigue. In the 70s, we were lucky if we had 15 players to use for a whole campaign. This again is directly linked towards changing attitudes towards injuries and rehabilitation.

In 1980, we were going for the title and were in the semi-final of the FA Cup against Arsenal. We played on the Saturday at Anfield, went to Villa Park on the Wednesday for the semi and extra time. Then we went to Palace on the Saturday and back to Villa Park on the Monday for 90 minutes and extra time before another game at Highfield Road on the Thursday to play Arsenal again. By the end of the second week, we didn't train on the Friday. Bob Paisley felt that it was better if we went for a walk. But few of the players could even walk. We'd used the same 13 players in all the games.

Some players get a runny nose now and they don't play. That's not really a reflection on the player. It's because all the players in each squad are so fit, if they aren't 100%, it shows in their match performance against other players that are 110% fit so the club's choose to pull them out of the squad.

In 1981, we played three games over Christmas and I couldn't walk. I was so tired, battered and bruised, but I didn't complain because I wanted to keep my place in the team. It showed in my performance because by the time we faced Wolves, I was told that their manager was shouting at their forwards to really have a go at me: "Play on the number 6…Hansen can't move," he yelled.

Bob Paisley wanted to give me a cortisone injection but I'd already had two in that season and there was a new ruling

In action during the
1988 FA Cup final

that limited the number of jabs you could have. So I played on regardless.

I remember another time when we were playing Benfica over in Lisbon in the European Cup. Me and Alan Kennedy had a few injury problems. On the morning of the game, we got into the lift in the team hotel and Joe Fagan jumped in with us. He had a sheet of paper in his hand with a pen. Casually, he just said: "Right lads, are you in or are you out?" I went, "erm…in." Al went: "In." It was unbelievable because I was really struggling and the pitch was heavy. In my mind, I'd decided that it was going to be too much for me but Joe didn't give me time to say no. We ended up going through in the tie, so everything turned out well.

There was a different occasion when I was out with a bad one and missed the League Cup final after going over on the Tuesday night before at Stoke. I was out for the following nine games. We won eight and drew one. I then played on a Tuesday night for the reserves at Preston and the first team played on the Wednesday at Old Trafford against Man Utd. I wasn't in the squad because I was still recovering, but I went along to show my support for the team. Then before leaving home for the ground, I cut my knee open when I dropped a glass in the kitchen. It needed 10 stitches and I was in agony.

I'd played in the middle of the park on the Tuesday night to get fitter and Roy Evans was calling me the "midfield maestro." When I arrived at Old Trafford, he kept on calling me it, but I said: "I'm not a midfield maestro anymore…look at my knee." I told them what happened but nobody said a word.

They beat Man United to extend their great run in the league, and I went into training on the Thursday and none of the management would look at me. I was still in pain.

On the Saturday, we were playing Man City at home, then Joe Fagan said to me: "Do you want to play?" We'd just gone on this amazing run and I wouldn't have expected to be anywhere near the team even if I was fit, but Joe and the rest of the people knew how to work a player's head when it came to injuries. They'd always take you by surprise. In the end, they left Terry McDermott out of the team and the run continued. He wasn't over-enamoured with the decision.

That's not saying that injuries didn't affect the Liverpool team, because they did. The best side I played in was the 1978/79, 1979/80 team that won the league in both seasons by a country mile, playing great football and scoring lots of goals. We played Dynamo Tblisi and got knocked out because we had three or four injuries. The beating we got over there was deserved but if we had some of those injured players in the squad, we may have knocked them out and gone on to collect another European Cup.

I don't know whether management at other clubs had the same attitude towards injuries in the sense that when you talk to opposing players, it's probably the last thing you want to talk about. Even on international duty.

Having said that, I think there were a certain generation of people involved in football that frowned upon injuries. It was like they thought there was something deeply wrong with you as a person if you were injured. I remember Reuben Bennett when I first arrived at the club. He was a great character. He always told the story when he got carried off to hospital at Dundee with a broken leg, before climbing through the turnstile and returning to the game. The players would laugh and joke about it, but he was deadly serious. All he'd talk about was how tough he was and how all the players in his day were a lot harder.

One of the most dangerous and at the same time funniest injuries I witnessed was when David Johnson banged his head in an FA Cup replay against Arsenal at Villa Park. He went off with concussion and came back on with a bandage round his head. He was a centre-forward but Bob Paisley told him to play on the wing. It was the best he ever played.

Dave didn't know where he was but there's a story going

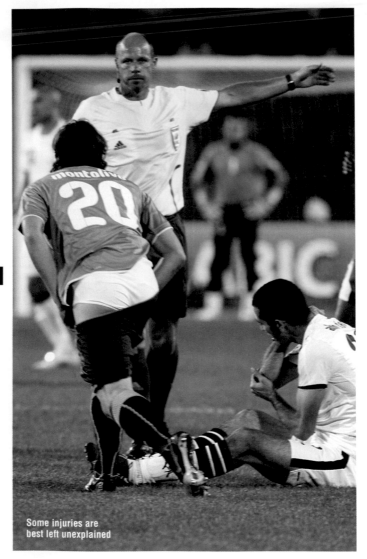

Some injuries are
best left unexplained

round that Bob Paisley said, "tell him he's Pele and get him back on there." That would have been typical of Bob. The funny thing about David Johnson was that his nickname was Doc. Even today, he still gets called that by all the lads. He had a medical bag with every kind of pill and tablet under the sun.

A football dressing room is a ruthless place and if you show any weakness at all, your team-mates will jump on it. So if your nickname is the Doc, then you get injured, like David, you're going to be in trouble.

There was also a funny moment at Crystal Palace when Phil Thompson did his shoulder. Ray Clemence came for a cross and took Tommo with him. There was a lot of reorganisation and we were in a mini-crisis trying to sort out the formation because we only had one recognised centre-back on the pitch. Palace were putting us under a lot of pressure and it looked like we might concede a goal. Instructions were coming from the bench but we couldn't hear them because the crowd was getting up for it and it was really noisy.

We managed to relieve some of the pressure and David Fairclough was taking the corner. He took his time over it to allow us to reorganise properly. Now many people remember Davey as the supersub who scored that great goal against Saint Etienne. But if you ask any of the Liverpool squad from that time about Davey, they'll all recall this story.

There were 22,000 fans in the ground and 22 players. The atmosphere was really tense but then David lightened the mood by running up, missing the ball and kicking the corner flag. He was nowhere near the ball and it didn't move an inch. Everyone on the pitch was in stitches. It was frighteningly funny. He needed treatment on his toe, but he was okay in the end.

If you think that was an absolute belter, that's nothing compared to some of the bizarre incidents coming up.

Enjoy the rest of the book – just make sure you don't injure yourself laughing...

No.1

YOU'RE NOT STINGING ANYMORE

JULIO ARCA, SUNDERLAND
Venue: Seaburn, North Sea

WING-BACK Julio Arca made headlines after suffering stings at the hands (or should that be tentacles?) of a Portuguese Man of War in August 2004. Ironically, the incident occurred when the players were taking a dip in the North Sea after training – swimming in the cold water is meant to prevent injuries.

Arca, who was stung in the chest, suffered an allergic reaction after initial treatment at Sunderland's training ground, but quickly recovered after being admitted to hospital. He should count himself fortunate – severe reactions can cause difficulty breathing, coma and even death.

There's an old wives' tale that says the only way to relieve the immediate pain from a jellyfish sting is by urinating on the victim's affected area. Whether or not his then manager Mick McCarthy understood this and decided to administer some 'emergency treatment' to his Argentinian left-footer is uncertain. McCarthy later joked: "The police officer who came down to deal with us said they've put out an APB on a black and white jellyfish."

Arca, meanwhile, made a full recovery in time to take part in a campaign that culminated in Sunderland's relegation from the Premier League. He has since moved on to Middlesbrough, where they too have suffered relegation to the Championship.

No.2

BACKYARD BLUNDER

FABIO AURELIO, LIVERPOOL
Venue: Back Garden

DESPITE consolidating his position as Liverpool's first-choice left-back during the 2008/09 season, Fabio Aurelio's three years at Anfield have been tempered by injury. Any run of form for the Reds has been abruptly terminated by an untimely fitness setback.

Aurelio's luck with injury was summed up in June 2009. Like many of the Liverpool squad not on international duty, he spent the summer with his family in the relative hazard-free haven of his back garden in his homeland of Brazil.

But while enjoying a leisurely kick-about with his son Fabio junior, Aurelio twisted his knee and was promptly ruled out for the beginning of Liverpool's new campaign.

The Brazilian is not a lone sufferer of garden provoked injuries, though. A 1998 survey by the Department of Trade and Industry revealed that 64,000 injuries take place in British gardens every year.

Celestine Babayaro fails to learn from his mistakes

022

Lomana LuaLua, preparing for lift-off

No.**3**

WHAT'S WRONG WITH A FIRM HANDSHAKE?

CELESTINE BABAYARO, CHELSEA
Venue: Broadhall Way, Stevenage

LOMANA LUALUA, PORTSMOUTH
Venue: Fratton Park, Portsmouth

CHELSEA spent a club record fee for a teenager when they paid Anderlecht £2.25m for **Celestine Babayaro** in 1997. But the Nigerian's over-enthusiastic somersault celebration in a pre-season friendly at Stevenage Borough resulted in a broken leg, ruling him out for the first six months of his debut season in west London.

Injury followed Babayaro throughout his career. He was released from Los Angeles Galaxy in 2007 by their coach Ruud Gullit without playing a competitive game. In his only appearance against FC Seoul in a friendly, he was booked and gave away a penalty – before suffering further injury setbacks.

Like Babayaro, **Lomana LuaLua**, the former Newcastle United and Portsmouth striker, injured himself showing off with a somersault celebration.

He twisted his ankle after a trademark multiple back-flip following a goal against Arsenal in April 2006. His manager at the time, Harry Redknapp, subsequently commented: "He still did his triple somersault with pike without realising he'd hurt himself." LuaLua moved to Al-Arabi in Qatar in 2008, after a spell in Greece with Olympiakos.

024

No. 4

READING MATTER

ALAN BALL, SOUTHAMPTON
Venue: Home dressing room, The Dell, Southampton

IN what was dubbed his farewell appearance in the Football League, the 1966 World Cup winner wasn't going to let the small matter of a broken toe banish his hopes of playing against Everton in October 1982, the club at which he won the league title 12 years before.

Just half-an-hour before kick-off, Ball, then 37, was walking barefoot to the toilet whilst reading a copy of *The Sporting Life*. His wife Leslie revealed: "He was concentrating so intently on picking the winners that he stubbed the smallest toe on his right foot on the wall."

In agony, the diagnosis was a break – but Ball still played after two pain-killing injections. Leslie added: "There was quite a crack. Danny Wallace, who was standing nearby, heard it quite clearly. Not surprisingly, the language was a bit special." Ball missed a penalty in the match, but was influential in a 3-2 victory.

026

Gordon Banks on England duty –
rogue foodstuffs not pictured

No.5

WHEN FOOD AND DRINK GOES BAD

GORDON BANKS, ENGLAND & STOKE CITY
Venue: Leon, Guanajuato, Mexico

TEN TOTTENHAM HOTSPUR PLAYERS
Venue: London Marriott Hotel, West India Quay

RONALDO
Venue: Stade de France, Paris

GORDON BANKS was declared unfit for the 1970 World Cup quarter-final against West Germany owing to a case of 'upset stomach'. Rather than consuming fish fingers like the rest of the squad, Banks had apparently eaten some sausages. His inclusion was still thought possible – until he keeled over in the middle of the team talk in the dressing room prior to kick-off.

027

It was later claimed that England manager Sir Alf Ramsey commented: "Of all the players we had to lose, it had to be him."

Ramsey marked Banks' importance to the squad ahead of fellow World Cup winners Bobby Moore, Bobby Charlton, Alan Ball and Geoff Hurst. And his absence against the Germans told.

With England 2-0 up, Banks' replacement, Peter Bonetti, allowed a shot from Franz Beckenbauer to slip underneath his body before Gerd Muller and Uwe Seeler secured an unlikely victory.

Conspiracies emerged, claiming that Banks had his food spiked by unscrupulous German dignitaries, but this claim was

Mystery illness – Where the
Tottenham 10 suffered

dismissed by the player in question, who watched the game on his hotel television and saw England go 2-0 ahead.

After a visit to the bathroom, he returned to bed and, feeling rough and sleepy, switched off his TV set to take a nap, assuming the match was won. He was woken by his second understudy, Alex Stepney, who came to his room to signal the final score with his fingers. West Germany had beaten England 3-2. Three days later, the reigning Labour government under Harold Wilson would lose the general election.

Banks' incident isn't the only example of mysterious circumstances surrounding the absence of a player, or a group of players, in an important match. **Ten Tottenham Hotspur players** fell ill at the team hotel just hours before the final game of the 2005/06 season, a crucial Premier League fixture with West Ham United.

Spurs needed three points to secure a Champions League place instead of north London rivals Arsenal. But less than 90

Spurs boss Martin Jol reflects on what might have been at Upton Park

Ronaldo in the team photo prior to the World Cup final in 1998

minutes before kick-off, Robbie Keane, Edgar Davids, Michael Dawson, Aaron Lennon, Michael Carrick, Teemu Tainio, Radek Cerny, Tom Huddlestone, Lee Barnard and Calum Davenport were struck down with illness. It was later discovered that the players were suffering from food poisoning. Spurs lost the match 2-1. The hotel was later cleared of any wrongdoing in the preparation, storage and cooking of food. Tests on the players found that one had a form of gastroenteritis, which may have spread to the other players affected.

In 1998, a puzzling episode surrounded **Ronaldo's** place in the Brazil team for the World Cup final against France. Boss Mario Zagallo initially omitted his star man from the starting XI, with Edmundo named in his place, much to the surprise of the whole world. Ronaldo was later reinstated to the team.

Various theories were bandied about as to the reasons for the uncertainty. An ankle injury, an upset stomach or even poison were cited. Eventually the official line was that the striker endured a funny turn in the team hotel hours before the kick-off, and Zagallo decided he wasn't mentally fit to start.

He eventually did, but France won the game 3-0 thanks to an inspirational performance from Zinedine Zidane.

The Brazilian superstar considers
what might have been in the
aftermath of the final in 1998

031

032

Steve Morrow receives attention after Arsenal's League Cup victory celebrations had turned sour – for the suited Anders Limpar, a scowl alone is not enough

No.

GOALS – BAD FOR YOUR HEALTH

STEFAN BARLIN, DJURGARDENS
Venue: Rasunda Stadium, Solna, Stockholm

CLAUS THOMSEN, EVERTON
Venue: Goodison Park, Liverpool

PAULO DIOGO, SERVETTE
Venue: Stadion Breite, Schaffhausen

YOUSSEF CHIPPO, COVENTRY CITY
Venue: Deepdale, Preston

THIERRY HENRY, ARSENAL
Venue: Highbury, London

SHAUN GOATER, MANCHESTER CITY
Venues: Britannia Stadium, Stoke & Maine Road, Manchester

STEVE MORROW, ARSENAL
Venue: Wembley Stadium, London

MOST goal-celebrating injuries can be linked to choreographed routines (see Celestine Babayaro). If you're **Stefan Barlin** though, they are suffered while expressing unforeseen pleasure. The left-winger, renowned for his pace rather than his goalscoring record, grabbed a decisive strike for Djurgardens in their derby victory against Hammarby in 2001, before over-exerting a muscle in his leg while running towards fans.

However, he isn't the only player to injure himself while celebrating an unexpected goal. In 1997, when Dave Watson netted a crucial winner for Everton against Derby County as they struggled against relegation, Danish midfielder **Claus Thomsen** managed to floor himself while embracing his team-mates. The stretcher-bearers were called, but he returned to the team a week later in the club's 2-0 defeat to Manchester United.

Thomsen was lucky compared to **Paulo Diogo**. The midfielder was playing for Servette in December 2004 when he jumped into the crowd to celebrate a goal against FC Schaffhausen – scored by team-mate Jean Beausejour. Unfortunately, he got his wedding ring caught on the fence and ripped off the top half of his finger. He also received a booking for his troubles. He revealed: "When I jumped down from the fence, I didn't feel anything at all. The first time I noticed that something was missing from my hand was when it started to hurt. And it hurt tremendously. I'm not dead and life goes on. So I have to live with one less finger."

Marcus Hall had scored only two goals for Coventry City at the start of the 2009/10 season, so it's ironic to recall a

Stefan Barlin

Claus Thomsen in action for Everton

Youssef Chippo looks to get his own back – while (inset) a lucky escape for Dion Dublin as Marcus Hall hails a City goal

035

bizarre injury related to one of the defender's two strikes, scored against Preston North End in September 2000. Hall put the Sky Blues two-up on the stroke of half-time in the League Cup second round, first-leg clash. The subsequent celebrations provided a casualty though, in the form of **Youssef Chippo**. Hall accidently poked the Moroccan in the eye – an injury that would force the midfielder off early in the second period. City at least came away with a 3-1 victory.

Ill-fated celebrations have affected better players, too. In 2000, **Thierry Henry** required treatment after hitting himself in the face with a corner flag following his, and the Gunners' second goal against Chelsea.

Two years earlier, fellow striker **Shaun Goater** (although not in the same class as Henry), having netted in a crucial match at Stoke City, fell on his arm in celebration – and broke it. Then

Thierry Henry maintains a firm grip on an offending Highbury corner flag (above), while Shaun Goater pictured in happier times – avoiding injury

Steve Morrow in the aftermath of his final fall

037

in 2003, he was forced off with a knee injury after celebrating a Nicolas Anelka goal against Birmingham – he had kicked an advertising hoarding.

Perhaps the most famous instance of a player injuring himself while celebrating is that of **Steve Morrow** when he scored the winner in the League Cup final of 1993.

The Northern Irishman broke his collarbone after falling off Tony Adams' shoulders in the celebrations following the 2-1 victory over Sheffield Wednesday. He was whisked off to hospital under the influence of laughing gas to numb the pain – without getting his hands on the trophy, or receiving a medal.

Morrow missed the rest of the season, including the FA Cup final (also against Wednesday), where Arsenal completed the domestic cup double after a dramatic replay. Before the final, Morrow finally received his League Cup winners' medal – becoming the only player to pick up a medal before a cup final.

He left his post as manager of FC Dallas in Major League Soccer in 2008.

Darren Barnard fails to heed the ref's warning

Liam Lawrence forgets where the dog lies

No. 7

MAN'S BEST FRIEND?

DARREN BARNARD, BARNSLEY
Venue: Unknown

LIAM LAWRENCE, STOKE CITY
Venue: Lawrence residence stairs

KEVIN HOFLAND, FEYENOORD
Venue: A park in Holland

JULIEN ESCUDE, RENNES
Venue: A park in France

CARLO CUDICINI, CHELSEA
Venue: A park in London

FRIEDEL RAUSCH, SCHALKE
Venue: Unknown

THE then Barnsley full-back **Darren Barnard** damaged knee ligaments after slipping on a puddle of his puppy's urine during the 1998/99 season. The incident is pretty embarrassing, but Barnard isn't alone in suffering a K9-inflicted injury.

Only back in 2008, winger **Liam Lawrence** of Stoke City tripped over his dog while walking down the stairs, suffering an ankle injury. He told reporters: "It was in the middle of the night, the dog lies on the stairs and I didn't see him. I trod on him, realised what I'd done, tried to go to the next step but went over on my ankle and fell down the stairs."

In the same year, **Kevin Hofland** of Dutch side Feyenoord missed a league clash with ADO Den Haag, owing to an ankle injury picked up walking his dog. "You have to ask Kevin's dog why he didn't participate in today's match," said coach Gert Jan Verbeek. "The dog wanted to go to the left and Kevin wanted to go to the right. This didn't work out too well for his ankle."

In 2002, **Julien Escude**, then of Rennes, damaged knee ligaments while walking his dog – he was ruled out for two months. He was most recently at Sevilla after a spell at Ajax.

A year earlier, Chelsea goalkeeper Carlo Cudicini tweaked his knee and required surgery after walking his dog. "I don't know whether his dog is a Rottweiler or a Pekinese, but Carlo was out walking it and it must have seen a rabbit or something because it gave him a sharp tug," Chelsea assistant manager Gwyn Williams told the national press.

Perhaps the most painful injury sustained courtesy of an unfriendly pooch came in 1969 when **Friedel Rausch**, then of Schalke, was bitten on the backside by a guard's German shepherd dog.

Julien Escude

Carlo Cudicini

Friedel Rausch, finding life
safer from the sidelines

041

Protesting Manchester United fans
maintain a safe distance from a
potentially dangerous pooch

David Batty on the look-out
for dangerous toddlers

TODDLERS CAN BE TROUBLE

DAVID BATTY, LEEDS UNITED
ALLAN NIELSEN, TOTTENHAM HOTSPUR
SEAN FLYNN, KIDDERMINSTER HARRIERS
ALAN MCLOUGHLIN, PORTSMOUTH
DAVE ROBINSON, HALIFAX TOWN
Venues: Unknown

IT'S ironic that former England international and notorious hardman David Batty was injured by a toddler on a tricycle. Batty was known as a motorbike enthusiast and often spent his time off racing around the Yorkshire Dales with friends, without ever bringing himself to any harm.

But when he rejoined Leeds United for a second spell at Elland Road in 1998, boss David O'Leary had it stipulated in his contract that he couldn't ride bikes in his spare time anymore. Batty was then promptly injured when his son rode a tricycle into his leg, damaging his Achilles tendons.

Batty, who also played for Blackburn Rovers and Newcastle United, remains the only player to be sent off in his last game for England – in a European Championship qualifier against Poland in 1999 – but he isn't the only player to suffer at the hands of a dangerous toddler.

In October 1996, not long after moving to Tottenham from Danish champions Brondby, **Allan Nielsen** was ruled out for several matches after his daughter poked him in the eye. He was forced off at half-time during a League Cup victory over Sunderland, with his then manager Gerry Francis revealing: "He had a problem with his retina. He went to see his new-born baby in hospital and the baby stuck something in Allan's eye. We seem to be inventing them [injuries] in all sorts of different ways." Nielsen later scored for Spurs in their League Cup final victory over Leicester in 1999.

Sean Flynn, the former Kidderminster Harriers captain, broke his nose and suffered a bust lip and bruised toes after tripping over his son's toy cars, and **Alan McLoughlin**, who features prominently later in this book in an incident involving John Durnin, once ruptured a muscle in his thumb when he picked up his daughter.

Defender **Dave Robinson** (below left) suffered the ignominy of putting his shoulder out falling off a kids' slide – he subsequently missed the start of the season for his club.

Alan McLoughlin and thumbs, in happier times

047

No.9

EASY RIDER

PETER BEAGRIE, EVERTON
Venue: Hotel Costa-Vasca, San Sebastian, Spain

THE winger drove a motorbike into a plate-glass window on Everton's 1991 pre-season tour in northern Spain. Having enjoyed a cold drink or 12 following a game against Real Sociedad, Beagrie flagged down a local motorcyclist, who gave him a lift back to the hotel. Unable to wake the night porter, he commandeered the bike, rode it up the hotel steps and straight through the glass doors. He required at least 40 stitches to a gashed left arm. Boss Howard Kendall was also forced to shell out £400 to the owner of the bike to pay for damage.

Quite how Beagrie didn't injure himself during a 20-year career spent executing a trademark somersault celebration whenever he scored is unbelievable. The injury he sustained in the pre-tee-total days of Premier League football, though, is rather more predictable.

In 2002, the UK national estimate for accidents while on holiday overseas was 480,664, with more than 5,000 of them fatal. Today, more than 800,000 people a year are being admitted to hospital with alcohol-related injuries.

Despite the severity of wounds on Beagrie's face and body, he was able to return to the Everton team quickly, with the Blues finishing the 1991/92 league season in 12th.

050

No.10

IF YOU CAN'T STAND THE HEAT...

DAVE BEASANT, CHELSEA
Venue: The Beasant residence

SANTIAGO CANIZARES, SPAIN
Venue: A hotel in Asia

DARREN BENT, CHARLTON ATHLETIC
Venue: The Bent residence

051

GOALKEEPER **Dave Beasant** didn't enjoy the best of spells at Chelsea, a period which saw him make errors both on and off the pitch. The 1988 FA Cup winner once dropped a jar of salad cream on his foot, severing the tendon in his big toe. He was out of action for two months.

He later revealed: "It was pre-season and I was going into a pantry cupboard at home to get something out, and my elbow knocked over this jar of salad cream. Both my hands were holding onto things, so my natural reaction was to stick out my foot to stop the jar hitting the floor. Unfortunately, I wasn't wearing any shoes or socks, and so when the jar hit my foot I got a nasty cut. It went right down to the bone and injured the ligaments underneath. It sounds funny but it ended up the most serious injury I had in my entire career and I was out for two-and-a-half months."

Beasant became a statistic in 1993. Like 85% of people who experience an injury in the kitchen, he severely cut at least one part of his body. Surprisingly, though, it was his foot. He was the antithesis of a modern-day sweeper keeper, so it's not surprising his footwork in the kitchen left as much to be desired as it did on the football pitch.

In the same year, former England international team-mate Gary Lineker was also suffering with a toe injury that would eventually end his career, so Beasant was only too aware of the perils that accompany such knocks.

Toe woe for Gary Lineker in the early 1990s

Dave Beasant
sees salad cream
in the distance

Darren Bent bears the scars of his onion episode

Years later, ahead of the 2002 World Cup held in Japan and South Korea, fellow goalkeeper **Santiago Canizares** severed a tendon in his big toe after trying to control a bottle of aftershave that fell from his hotel sink. The glass shattered, and Canizares missed the tournament with Spain.

In 2006, **Darren Bent** injured himself in the kitchen while chopping onions. Then a Charlton Athletic player, Bent cut his finger, tearing a tendon, and missed a pre-season friendly. They say chopping onions brings a tear to the eye. It certainly did on this occasion for the former Ipswich and Tottenham striker.

056

No.11

BOOTS AND ALL

DAVID BECKHAM, MANCHESTER UNITED
Venue: Old Trafford, Manchester

WHEN you get determined characters like Sir Alex Ferguson and David Beckham going head to head, sparks fly – and so do football boots. Beckham suffered a nasty facial injury during a dressing room incident at Old Trafford in 2003. United had just been knocked out of the FA Cup by Arsenal and tempers were running high, when a furious Fergie sent a stray boot flying through the air in the direction of his star midfielder. Beckham emerged sporting a criss-cross bandage over his left eyebrow. A club spokesman commented: "These things happen. They are both grown men and I'm sure they will move on from here."

The wound healed in a matter of weeks but it's fair to say that things were never the same between Becks and Fergie – the England captain left United for Real Madrid in a £24.5m deal just a few months later.

Christian Okpala (above)
– gassy victim, and
Duncan Ferguson

058

No.12

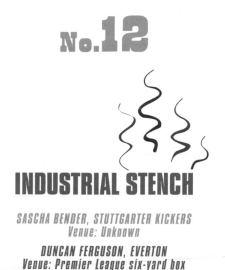

INDUSTRIAL STENCH

SASCHA BENDER, STUTTGARTER KICKERS
Venue: Unknown

DUNCAN FERGUSON, EVERTON
Venue: Premier League six-yard box

059

SASCHA BENDER suffered a face injury thanks to passing wind in 2006. His team-mate Christian Okpala had punched him, offering the following explanation to the media: "He permanently provoked me by farting all the time." The issue had apparently grown when the duo were team-mates at previous club FC Augsburg.

Bender isn't the only player to gain notoriety for flatulence. Allegedly, former Everton striker **Duncan Ferguson** once managed to clear the six-yard box while attacking a corner after breaking wind in a Premier League match. Unsurprisingly Ferguson, who previously spent time in the nick following an on-pitch confrontation with an opponent, was not apprehended for his mischievous deed on this occasion.

Meteorologists in America recorded 70 wind-related deaths in 2008, more than doubling the 2007 total of 34, while in Britain figures suggest that there were close to 20,000 accidents caused by gas in 2005.

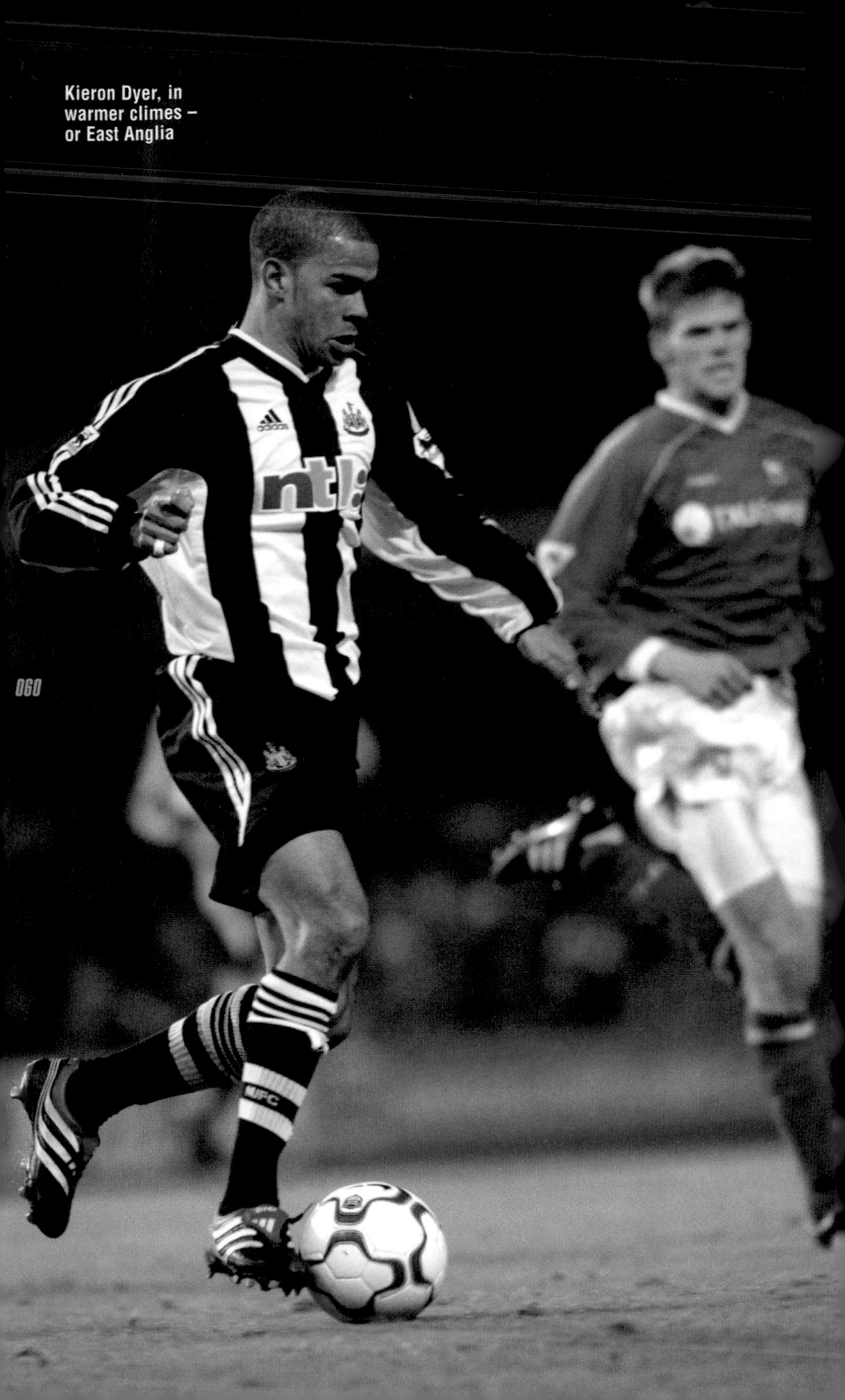

Kieron Dyer, in warmer climes – or East Anglia

COLD SNAP

MIKE BENNETT, ST PHILIP'S
Venue: Unknown

KIERON DYER, NEWCASTLE UNITED
Venue: North East England

A GOALKEEPER for Bristol team St Philip's, Mike Bennett made no attempt to save a shot during a game in the 1989/90 season. The reason was soon discovered – he was suffering from hypothermia.

The hypothermia will have been bad enough, but after such a static performance where he undoubtedly conceded a number of goals, Bennett will have been given the cold shoulder by his team-mates as well.

Kieron Dyer has endured his fair share of injury problems during his football career – and training ground woes, as is noted later. The cold of December in Newcastle brought on a case of frostbite in the midfielder in 2001. A metal rod inserted in his leg to cure a shin problem proved an adequate solution and he made his comeback for the Magpies as a substitute against former club Ipswich – until the sub-zero Tyneside temperatures intervened the following week, causing the niggle to re-occur in Dyer's shin.

Hypothermia is classified as a temperature below 35 degrees (96 Fahrenheit). In 2003, the NHS calculated that 74 percent of hypothermic episodes required hospital attention, while in the USA more than 600 people a year die from hypothermia.

Kieron Dyer reflects on a cold injury

No.14

I FEEL LIKE CHICKEN TONIGHT

IVANO BONETTI, GRIMSBY TOWN
Venue: Kenilworth Road, Luton

IVAN BONETTI surprised the football world in 1995 when he moved from Torino – the fifth most successful club in Italian football – to Grimsby Town, then in the old Second Division. In an era when Italian football was as vogue as a peroxide blonde hairdo amongst Premier League footballers, Bonetti was one of few players to trade Serie A for England. Mariners' supporters, who had little to celebrate in their 117-year history, rejoiced and Bonetti became an instant favourite on the terraces.

Their loyalty was soon tested, though, when it was announced that £100,000 was needed to retain Bonetti from the American management company that held the rights to his 'services and image'. Such was Bonetti's contentment on the banks of the Humber, he stumped up £50,000 of his own cash to make the deal possible, thus increasing his appeal at Blundell Park even further.

Ivano Bonetti signs on the dotted line at Grimsby

The unlikely love-in between the Italian and Lincolnshire folk was made unconditional when the Brescia-born midfielder scored the winning goal against West Bromwich Albion – then managed by former Grimsby boss Alan Buckley, and a side that featured several former Mariners players.

A whirlwind romance ended in heartbreak though, when Bonetti fell out with boss Brian Laws in February 1996. Laws unintentionally broke the Italian's cheekbone when he threw a plate of chicken wings at him in a dressing room row following a 3-2 defeat at Luton Town – Town had beaten them 7-1 in the FA Cup a month before.

The chicken incident resulted in Bonetti moving to Tranmere Rovers, where he played for a season before spells at Crystal Palace and Genoa. He returned to Britain in 2000 to play in Scotland for Dundee.

Bonetti came third in the BBC's Grimsby 'cult heroes' poll in 2004, after playing fewer than 30 games for the club. He finished behind Clive Mendonca (61 league goals) and John McDermott (over 600 league appearances).

When chicken wings attack – Ivano bears the scars

No.15

DON'T ANSWER THE PHONE

NIGEL BOOGAARD, CENTRAL COAST MARINERS
Venue: Boogaard residence

INJURY and illness have been big factors in Australian defender Nigel Boogaard's football career so far. A groin strain picked up answering his phone has done little to suggest these problems will change any time soon. Having been ruled out for a few weeks with concussion, the player was resting at home when his phone went off in December 2007. His coach Lawrie McKinna revealed: "He jumped up to get it [the phone]. He then slipped on the tiles at his home and strained his groin. I'm serious – I'm not joking!"

Nigel Boogaard feeling the strain on the pitch, as well as off it

No.16

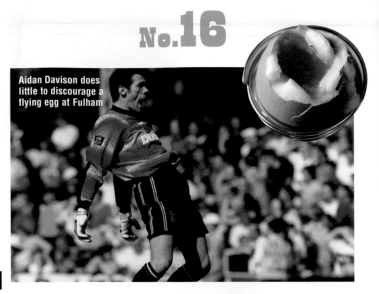

Aidan Davison does little to discourage a flying egg at Fulham

EGG IN YOUR FACE

KIRK BROADFOOT, RANGERS
Venue: Broadfoot household

AIDAN DAVISON, GRIMSBY TOWN
Venue: Craven Cottage, Fulham

IN 2004, boffins in the UK said that microwave ovens should display prominent warnings about the dangers of exploding eggs. Experts made the appeal in a letter to the British Medical Journal. The letter described the case of a nine-year-old girl who reheated a boiled egg in a microwave for 40 seconds. About 30 seconds later, when she was carrying the egg, it exploded, hitting her in the right eye and face.

The shrapnel from the scalding egg tore open her cornea, the transparent coating that covers the iris and pupil, and caused the lens of her eye to cloud over so she could see only hand movements. Several months later, her vision was restored, but only after two operations in which her cornea was stitched and her damaged lens replaced with a plastic one. The recommendation came after a 2001 review of the medical literature turned up 13 cases in which microwaved eggs exploded and caused injuries, mostly burns.

Luckily for peckish Gers full-back **Kirk Broadfoot**, who was poaching the offending egg in the microwave before scalding hot liquid squirted onto his face, his injuries weren't so serious and he soon returned to training – where he was greeted with a barrage of egg-related abuse in 2009. He later revealed how he could have lost his sight. "There was boiling water and glass in my face."

Broadfoot isn't the only player to suffer at the expense of an over-active oeuf. In 1998, Grimsby Town goalkeeper **Aidan Davison** was felled by a hard-boiled version during a Second Division play-off game against Fulham.

069

Kirk Broadfoot (right) celebrates
winning the Scottish title in 2009

Shaun Teale,
in safer times

No.17

BAD ANIMALS

CHIC BRODIE, BRENTFORD
Venue: Griffin Park, Brentford

SVEIN GRONDALEN, NORWAY
Venue: Moose-friendly land in Norway

MISTAR, INDONESIA
Venue: Training pitch, Indonesia

SHAUN TEALE, ASTON VILLA
Venue: Teale Towers

071

CHIC BRODIE'S professional career was ended in bizarre fashion in November 1970. Another player that could have been added to the 'Man's Best Friend?' category, goalkeeper Brodie suffered at the paws of a four-legged 'friend'. Said dog had 'invaded' Brentford's Griffin Park pitch and having followed where the ball was travelling, the less than loveable pooch collided with Brodie's knee as he bent down to pick the ball up. He was subsequently stretchered off, and never played competitively for the Bees again.

Given the number of curious injuries Brodie suffered during his career – which included a hand grenade being thrown into his goalmouth, and the entire goal collapsing around him in another match – you would think he was the unluckiest footballer in the world. But he is not alone.

Sometime in the 1970s, **Svein Grondalen**, a Norwegian defender, was forced to miss an international match when he collided with a moose while out jogging. The almost comical nature of the injury was made even more amusing by the fact that Grondalen was a defender noted for his brute strength. Many Scandinavians of a certain vintage remember him best for a reckless tackle, which injured Swede Ralf Edstrom during an international between the rival nations in 1977.

In 1995, tragedy struck 25-year-old Indonesian footballer **Mistar,** who was killed by a drove of stampeding pigs, which overran his team's training pitch before an Independence Cup fixture.

During his spell in the West Midlands, defender **Shaun Teale** suffered a serious gash to his forearm as a result of an accident, again involving a creature – although not directly. He was actually cleaning out the family fish tank.

No.18

GOALMOUTH ACTION

ROY CARROLL, WEST HAM UNITED
Venue: Various

PETER ENCKELMAN, BLACKBURN ROVERS
Venue: Germany

ANDREW BAIRD, QUEEN'S PARK
Venue: Glasgow

073

NORTHERN IRELAND international goalkeeper **Roy Carroll** once picked up a knee injury when he caught his foot in a goal net as he retrieved footballs.

Other incidents have followed Carroll throughout his career. No matter what he does in the future, he will always be known for the 'goal that never was' while playing for Manchester United against Tottenham Hotspur in 2005. Carroll dropped a speculative shot from Pedro Mendes well behind his goal-line, before scooping the ball back into play without the referee or his assistants realising it had gone in.

Prior to arriving at Old Trafford, Carroll was voted as the best goalkeeper in the Second Division by fellow professionals – a

Roy Carroll takes greater
care than usual in the net

feat made more impressive by the fact that he missed the last seven games of the league season after an emergency appendix operation.

While at Aston Villa, goalkeeper **Peter Enckelman** once let a throw-in from one of his own players slip under his foot and into the net. The unfortunate incident occurred at the ground of close city rivals Birmingham City, on live television. Calamitous goings-on continued while at Blackburn Rovers. A pre-season friendly in Germany in July 2006 against Olympiacos saw Rovers go down to a 5-0 defeat. Enckelman could hardly be blamed though – he missed the fixture after twisting his foot in the netting during the pre-match warm-up.

Andrew Baird's tale relates to a Scottish Cup semi-final tie against Rangers way back in 1894. Somehow the goalkeeper found himself in the humiliating position of having a hand caught in the netting – not an ideal situation when forward David Boyd is bearing down on goal. Boyd showed no mercy, and the Gers went through to beat Celtic in the final.

075

Peter Enckelman has no place to hide after the incident at St Andrew's

Matt Clarke (right)
celebrates Bradford's
great escape in 1999
with David Wetherall

076

No.19

ONE STEP BEYOND

MATT CLARKE, BRADFORD CITY
Venue: Clarke household

BRADFORD CITY'S first-choice stopper Matt Clarke, who had been recovering from injury, fell down stairs at his home before the Premier League clash with local rivals Leeds United at Valley Parade in 2000. With Gary Walsh and a certain Aidan Davison also on the books – but also injured – the transfer deadline passed with City apparently failing in a bid for Leeds' Paul Robinson. United were not keen on granting permission for him to play against his parent club, so the move collapsed. Too late to bring in a replacement, young stopper Danny Taylor (who now runs a hairdressing salon in Bradford) was set to make his bow, but was deemed too inexperienced. Thus coach Neville Southall, 41, was brought in – and City went down 2-1.

In 2000, it was revealed that more than 100,000 people were treated for injuries sustained on stairs, with 1,000 fatalities. Studies also suggested that impaired vision – a problem particularly if you're a goalkeeper – reduced strength, and poor balance put elderly people at particular risk (Clarke was 27 when he injured himself). Many accidents were also caused as a result of people leaving objects on stairs, or carrying difficult objects up and down them.

Clarke, meanwhile, who played an integral role in Bradford's escape from the Premier League relegation zone in 1999, later moved to Bolton Wanderers and Crystal Palace. Ironically, he also suffered a bizarre injury with the South London club after cutting his hand in a household accident.

He retired in 2004, with injury curtailing his career at the age of only 31. During his time as a Rotherham United player in the early 90s, Clarke had been known as Matt the Cat.

No.20

WHO'D BE A KEEPER?

RAY CLEMENCE, ENGLAND
Venue: Stadio Comunale, Turin

DIDA, AC MILAN
Venues: San Siro Stadium, Milan & Parkhead, Glasgow

BRUCE GROBBELAAR, ZIMBABWE
Venue: Unknown

ROBBIE SIMPSON, CELTIC
Venue: Avellaneda, Buenos Aires, Argentina

FORMER Liverpool goalkeeper **Ray Clemence** was forced to leave the field for a brief spell after reacting to tear gas let off by Italian police. "Drunken, brawling" England fans had begun causing chaos during the opening European Championship match against Belgium in June 1980. Trouble had broken out on the terraces behind Clemence's goal, apparently after Belgium's Jan Ceulemans had netted a 29th-minute equaliser, only four minutes after Ray Wilkins had opened the scoring. Fortunately there would be no further goals in the group game.

The fixture was subsequently held up for five minutes after the goalkeeper apparently collapsed choking, the tear gas having drifted across the field. It also affected full-back Kenny Sansom, both players seen to wipe their eyes and being unable to see for a short period. The FA would receive an £8,000 fine as a result of the scenes.

Tear gas and flares were not just a fad of the 1980s though. In 2005, with AC Milan leading 1-0 in the second leg of the Champions League quarter-final derby against cross-town rival Internazionale, Inter ultras became infuriated after a second-half Esteban Cambiasso goal was ruled out by German referee Markus Merk who, moments later, booked Cambiasso for dissent. Bottles and debris were subsequently thrown onto the pitch, and the projectiles soon escalated to lit flares. As Brazilian goalkeeper **Dida** attempted to clear bottles in order to take a goal-kick, a flare hurtled down from the upper deck and struck him on his right shoulder. Merk then halted the match.

Tear gas in Turin proved a problem for
England goalkeeper Ray Clemence

Dida on the San Siro turf
after being hit by a flare

After a 30-minute delay in which firefighters were called in to remove the burning flares from the pitch, the match was restarted. Dida, however, was unable to continue, and was substituted by Christian Abbiati. Less than a minute later though, Merk finally abandoned the match after more flares and debris rained down from the terraces.

Eventually, UEFA ruled a 3-0 victory to Milan while Dida suffered bruising and first-degree burns to his shoulder. He didn't miss a game, though, and returned to the Milan team the following weekend against Siena.

Two years later, Dida would be at the centre of another incident. He was found to have feigned injury, holding his face after being hit on the shoulder by a Celtic fan during a Champions League match. Dida was subsequently charged by UEFA with breaching rules upholding "loyalty, integrity and sportsmanship".

Bruce Grobbelaar aims to avoid flying objects

There are a number of other occasions when a goalkeeper has been the unfortunate victim of a missile-throwing crowd. In 1993, **Bruce Grobbelaar** – Ray Clemence's successor as Liverpool No. 1 – was injured following crowd violence. He was hit on the head with a rock during a World Cup qualifier while playing for Zimbabwe. He subsquently required a brain scan.

Legendary Celtic goalkeeper **Robbie Simpson** also missed the second leg of the 1967 Intercontinental Cup final against Racing. The then veteran Scotland international was struck on the head by a missile fired from the crowd just before kick-off and was subsequently knocked out, being forced to leave the pitch. For fear of a riot, Celtic played the match and lost 2-1, meaning a third match to decide the overall winners, the first leg having been won 1-0 by the Scottish club. In a particularly brutal play-off played in Montevideo, Simpson was left out due to his injury – the effects of which Celtic's manager Jock Stein felt would be psychological as well as physical. They would go on to lose the match 1-0.

Robbie Simpson diving at the feet of Ian St John at Anfield – Safer than Buenos Aires

084

Andy Goram in action and
(inset), Stan Collymore
feels the strain

No.21

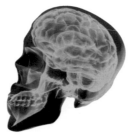

MAKING YOUR MIND UP

STAN COLLYMORE, ASTON VILLA
ANDY GORAM, SCOTLAND
Venue: In the head

085

WHEN Aston Villa striker **Stan Collymore** was diagnosed with clinical depression in 1998, boss John Gregory reportedly questioned how anybody being paid as handsomely as Collymore to play for his boyhood favourites could be depressed.

Managers have suggested that 99% of football matches are won in the head, and every year 19 million people succumb to clinical depression. In addition, figures suggest that up to 10% of women and 3-5% of men worldwide may be suffering from clinical depression at any given time.

The illness forced Scotland goalkeeper **Andy Goram** to miss the 1998 World Cup in France. The former Rangers stopper's condition was described as not "mentally attuned". After being treated for mild schizophrenia, Goram was playing at Dundee when the crowd allegedly chanted: "Two Andy Gorams, there's only two Andy Gorams..."

No.22

MAN AT HOME

GREGORY COUPET, LYON
Venue: Coupet household

JOHN 'JOCK' QUAIRNEY, ROTHERHAM UNITED
Venue: Quairney home

FRANCE international goalkeeper **Gregory Coupet** was ruled out of action for two weeks after cutting two of his fingers putting up a shelf.

Like most alpha males, Coupet probably considered himself a dab hand with a screwdriver. But like most men of a certain age, he suffered at the mercy of his tool.

It is estimated that a surge in injuries and even deaths among handymen is traditionally seen on Easter Bank Holiday Monday. In 1999, 1,400 people injured themselves over the Easter break – making it the most dangerous period in a year, with 200,000 DIY injuries and 70 deaths annually in Britain.

There are more than 200,000 accidents a year associated with work around the house. Most back pain is due to the prolonged stretching of tendons and ligaments in the back.

Generally, around 20 people a day are admitted to hospital after injuring themselves carrying out DIY repairs. The number of people hurt using non-powered hand tools such as saws and chisels has risen 104% from 2,124 in 1999 to 4,335. Power tool injuries increased 79% from 1,728 to 3,089 in 2008.

Coupet, meanwhile, recovered and was quickly restored to a Lyon team that would dominate French football for the best part of a decade. Incidentally, his only other serious injury at the club was in August 2007. He suffered knee ligament damage caused, like messrs Carroll, Enckelman and Baird, after getting caught in the goal net. He commented: "It's not the end of the world. The good side is that we have a rugby World Cup coming and I'll be able to enjoy every bit of it." He was most recently at Paris Saint Germain.

A near-miss also came to light concerning Rotherham United goalkeeper **John 'Jock' Quairney**. The Scottish goalkeeper almost missed his side's FA Cup tie with Bury in January 1952. Carving a Sunday joint the previous week, he cut his right hand. Fortunately, he passed a subsequent fitness test, helping his side to a 2-1 win.

087

Gregory Coupet –
DIY victim

Andy Dibble –
Grateful for a
knowledgeable
groundsman

088

No.23

CHEMICAL WORLD

ANDY DIBBLE, BARRY TOWN
Venue: Richmond Park, Carmarthen

JASON KOUMAS, WEST BROMWICH ALBION
Venue: The Hawthorns, West Bromwich

FULHAM PLAYERS
Venue: The Homelands, Ashford, Kent

089

THE veteran Wales goalkeeper **Andy Dibble** was hospitalised in December 1998 after suffering chemical burns as a result of diving on Carmarthen Town's Richmond Park surface. Making a loan appearance for Barry Town – he was on Altrincham's books at the time – it was discovered that the penalty spot he had slid on had been painted using lime.

Dibble's dabble with dangerous chemicals sounds horrific, but he was soon back playing with Wrexham – although maybe too early. Most similar accidents usually cause only first-degree burns and peel like a sunburn over the following week, yet Dibble's burns were bad and scarred him for life. He later received £20,000 in damages and was most recently working as a goalkeeping coach with Championship side Peterborough United.

Another player to suffer from injuries sustained by the pitch is another Welshman, **Jason Koumas**. He picked up an eye infection on his West Bromwich Albion debut in 2002, when he wiped fertiliser in his eye at the Hawthorns.

Fulham, then in today's equivalent of League One, snatched a 2-2 draw at non-leaguers Ashford Town in the first round of the FA Cup back in November 1994. Afterwards, three players apparently complained of blistering, pointing the finger at the half-time re-marking that had taken place on the pitch – with pure lime. The Cottagers would win the replay 5-3.

Jason Koumas takes a risk by sliding into a tackle on his West Brom debut

No.24

CADDY SHACK

JOHN DURNIN, PORTSMOUTH
Venue: Golf course

KASEY KELLER, LEICESTER CITY
Venue: Keller's car boot

MARK STATHAM, STALYBRIDGE CELTIC
Venue: Car

091

IT'S known that the most common golf injuries occur in the lower back, elbows, shoulders, hands and wrists and are generally defined as either cumulative (overuse) or acute (traumatic) injuries.

An improvement in swing technique is usually enough to help those that are plagued by such knocks. Careful driving when using a buggy is also advisable if you're **John Durnin**.

The former Liverpool striker, most noted for his time at Oxford United and Portsmouth, spent six weeks out after crashing his buggy into a fairway hollow and dislocating his elbow. 'Johnny Lager,' as he was known by Pompey fans,

Kasey Keller – Maybe he should have stuck with baseball

allegedly didn't see a ditch as he was admiring the view. "It could have been a lot worse and we're lucky to come out of it like we have," said witness and midfielder Alan McLoughlin. McLoughlin was right. In 2008, it was found that 10 people lost eyes in golf course accidents, according to eye specialists.

On that basis **Kasey Keller**, the former Leicester City goalkeeper who's most recent club is the Seattle Sounders in Major League Soccer, was one of the lucky ones. In 1998, he knocked out his front teeth pulling a golf bag from the boot of his car.

Although he may enjoy a round of golf, **Mark Statham's** injury had more to do with car judgement. The one-time Nottingham Forest goalkeeper was forced to miss a game in 1999 after apparently getting his head trapped – in a car door.

Emerson – Better outfield

094

No.25

TRAINING WOES

EMERSON, BRAZIL
Venue: Munsu Football Stadium, Ulsan, South Korea

KIERON DYER, NEWCASTLE UNITED & WEST HAM UNITED
Venue: Various

DEREK McINNES, WEST BROMWICH ALBION
Venue: Great Barr, Walsall

095

THE day before Brazil's 2002 World Cup opener against Turkey, **Emerson** took part in a relaxing training session, going in goal during a kickaround. However, he injured his shoulder, causing him to miss the tournament – and his country's success.

Unsurprisingly, more injuries are sustained by footballers on the training ground than in matchday action. Although impact knocks incurred from the common tackle are most frequent, players have often been found injuring themselves in a rather more unconventional manner. **Kieron Dyer**, for instance, when at Newcastle United suffered damage to his left eye after colliding with a pole in training.

Despite the comical nature of this injury, he was less lucky upon moving to West Ham United for £6m in 2007. After making his debut against Birmingham City, 10 days later he was stretchered off following a tackle by Joe Jacobson in a Carling Cup match against Bristol Rovers. It was found that his leg was broken in two places. Dyer subsequently missed the rest of the 2007/08 season and didn't return to the team until January 2009, in an FA Cup tie at Hartlepool United.

In 2002, West Bromwich Albion's **Derek McInnes** picked up an ankle injury while failing to negotiate a traffic cone in training. "It was a freak accident," said manager Gary Megson. "We use these traffic cones like a lot of clubs for training purposes and Derek jumped up to head a ball, came down and landed on the edge of it and twisted his ankle."

Derek McInnes – Trying to avoid cones since 2002

Kieron Dyer – Unlucky

097

No.26

HOME COMFORTS

LES FERDINAND, TOTTENHAM HOTSPUR
Venue: Chez Ferdinand

LEDLEY KING, TOTTENHAM HOTSPUR
Venue: Various

RIO FERDINAND, LEEDS UNITED
Venue: Rio Residence

JOHN TERRY, CHELSEA
Venue: Chelsea's training ground

ROBBIE KEANE, WOLVES
Venue: Keane Household

DEREK LYLE, DUNDEE
Venue: Lyle Residence

LES FERDINAND was ruled out for the rest of the season in April 2002 after breaking his wrist in a freak accident at home. "I was just messing about at home and toppled over. I fell awkwardly and my wrist seemed to take most of the weight", Les later told the media.

His misfortune at home could be attributed to a recent phenomenon known as 'toppling'. Toppling is defined as falling over from top-heaviness or lack of support. He probably succumbed to this occurrence due to his upper body strength. Renowned as a striker blessed with upward mobility, facing Ferdinand was a frightening prospect for any defender in the Premier League at his peak during the mid-1990s.

By the time he joined Spurs, though – a club that seems to have been plagued by injuries throughout this book – he was nearing the end of his career, and this could have resulted in him being less nimble on his feet.

It is surprising that another Tottenham player, **Ledley King**, hasn't been a victim of toppling, especially given his horrific injury record. In 2008, one national newspaper estimated that King had missed nearly four seasons' football with 22 different injuries.

Les isn't the only Ferdinand to experience unusual harm at home. Little cousin **Rio Ferdinand** pulled a muscle in January 2001 after watching television for too long by leaving his leg resting on a coffee table.

"It was a freak accident," revealed his then boss at Leeds United, David O'Leary. "It wasn't even on the training ground;

Ledley King

Rio Ferdinand –
Coffee table woes

101

Tim Henman congratulates Lleyton Hewitt in
2002 – while John Terry (inset) was in agony

he was watching television and had his foot up on the coffee table. He had it there in a certain position for a number of hours...and strained a tendon behind his knee." Ironically, he'd been following doctor's orders by resting.

A similar problem befell **John Terry**, although the Chelsea defender was watching TV in the comfort of the club's training ground. While watching Lleyton Hewitt beat Tim Henman at Wimbledon in July 2002, Terry apparently turned to a team-mate to chat, presumably about the match in progress. Unfortunately, this caused a knee injury, which required keyhole surgery. He later commented: "It's very disappointing, but the knee can't have been right before the mishap."

While a fledgling forward making his way at Wolves, **Robbie Keane** also damaged his ankle – standing on a remote control in 1998.

Dundee's **Derek Lyle** missed a game in 2008 when, like Rio, he succumbed to a coffee table, this time falling through his glass one at home – cutting his stomach in the process.

No.27

CREEPY CRAWLIES

104

ROWEN FERNANDEZ, KAIZER CHIEFS
Venue: Fernandez Residence

NICK HOLMES, SOUTHAMPTON
Venue: Unknown

GOALKEEPERS are meant to be different, and **Rowen Fernandez** certainly fulfills that criteria.

'Spider', as he is known to his team-mates, became a victim of his own infatuation when he was hospitalised in Johannesburg, South Africa. Fernandez had long been a lover of creepy crawlies – including snakes – when one of his eight-legged friends decided to feast on his arm in 2003.

It is believed that most spiders will avoid physical contact but when they are accidentally touched or squeezed, they can deliver a bite in self-defence. Given his fondness for the deadly creatures, maybe Fernandez hugged his pet with too much care, forcing it to pinch.

Rowen Fernandez – Added bite

Although it is estimated that between 98 and 99% of spider bites are harmless, the symptoms of their bites can include necrotic wounds, systemic toxicity and in some cases, death.

Fernandez recovered and became a full international in 2004, making his debut for South Africa against Tunisia. He is expected to feature in the 2010 World Cup held in his home country. He was most recently with Arminia Bielefeld in the German Bundesliga.

Midfielder **Nick Holmes** was a one-club man who made over 500 apperances for Southampton, helping them to FA Cup glory in 1976. A story goes that he was forced to take no part in a game for the club – after falling on an ants' nest.

Nick Holmes –
Ant victim

No.28

GENTS
HOMMES

TKO

DARREN FLETCHER, MANCHESTER UNITED
Venue: Fletcher home

PERRY GROVES, ARSENAL
Venue: Highbury, London

BEFORE Manchester United's Champions League success in 2008, some United fans would have said that **Darren Fletcher** was in a permanent state of unconsciousness because an unconscious person is usually completely unresponsive to their environment or people around them – something that for a long time plagued the player on the pitch.

After United's Champions League defeat of Lyon in March 2008, the midfielder attempted to swing a bathroom door open – when the door fell on his head, knocking him unconscious.

It seems to have knocked some sense into him because since then, the Scot has been an integral figure in Sir Alex Ferguson's midfield, featuring heavily in United's march to the

Darren Fletcher mulls over the case of the swinging door

108

double success of Premier League and Champions League in 2008, and again in the side that challenged on all five fronts 12 months later.

In September 1986, **Perry Groves** fulfilled a lifelong dream by signing for Arsenal. Yet to make an appearance for the club, he was apparently sat on the Gunners' bench when his new side scored a goal against Sheffield Wednesday. He jumped up to celebrate it, and unfortunately hit his head on the roof of the dugout, knocking himself out. He eventually received treatment from the physio.

Incidentally, more than half a million people in the UK are knocked unconscious every year in the UK.

Perry Groves on the pitch –
Less likely to do himself harm

Paul Gascoigne, complete with 'Phantom of the Opera' protection

110

No.29

THREE AND A BED

PAUL GASCOIGNE, LAZIO
Venue: Various

BRYAN ROBSON, ENGLAND
Venue: Hotel in Italy

LEROY LITA, READING
Venue: The Lita bed

GIVEN **Paul Gascoigne's** colourful career, it is perhaps surprising that he is only noted in this book for having strained a thigh getting out of his bed. Well, that and inadvertently ruling England's captain out of the majority of the 1990 World Cup, but more of that later.

The England star had reported back to his club side Lazio after a Christmas break in late 1993 with the injury news, only months after coming back a stone and a half overweight after his summer off. Despite well-documented weight troubles, Gazza had been relatively injury free until 1991. That was the year when he ruptured the cruciate knee ligaments in his right knee during Tottenham Hotspur's FA Cup final victory over Nottingham Forest.

Although the injury forced the delay of a proposed move to Serie A, he did eventually move to the Rome club in the summer of 1992. Fitness issues again proved a problem though, with a cheekbone injury in April 1993 forcing the midfielder to don an unusual 'Phantom of the Opera' mask to allow him to play in matches.

After retirement from football, Gascoigne has continued to be beset by fitness problems. In May 2008, his comeback in a charity match was wrecked by a rare foot injury.

Now in his early 40s, Gascoigne was due to play his first game since retiring five years before in a fundraiser for cash-strapped Darlington. But Gazza, who had been training in Newcastle United's gym, was struck down with "foot drop", a

A bed, yesterday – A danger to footballers

Bryan Robson played through the pain barrier during the 1990 World Cup

113

condition which prevents sufferers lifting their foot normally, and making them limp.

Then England skipper **Bryan Robson** was ruled out of much of Italia '90 due to lifting a bed – with a certain Paul Gascoigne on it. Consequently he lost his grip and the leg of the bed landed on his toe. Although he featured in England's first two group games against the Republic of Ireland and Holland courtesy of a pain-killing injection, a long-standing Achilles tendon problem would end his World Cup. 'Captain Marvel's' absence was critical. It not only deprived England of their captain and most influential player, it allowed other lesser-established players to forge a reputation on the international stage and secure moves to bigger clubs. Gascoigne and David Platt were just two.

It wasn't the first time Robson had missed games in a major tournament. He missed a game against Kuwait during the 1982 finals with a thigh problem, and in 1986 picked up a dislocated shoulder in the second game against Morocco, taking no further part in the competition as a result.

The absence of key players has been a major problem in the England squad during international competitions over the years. Of course, as has been noted there was Gordon Banks in 1970, while in 1982 usual skipper Kevin Keegan and Trevor Brooking were selected – despite travelling to Spain injured. Indeed, the pair only featured in the final second round group phase match against the hosts as second-half substitutes. In recent times Steven Gerrard missed the 2002 World Cup in Japan and South Korea because of injury. Wayne Rooney also limped out of the European Championships in Portugal two years later for the same reason. Then in '06, Michael Owen damaged the anterior cruciate ligament in his knee, forcing him to miss almost a year of football.

Forward **Leroy Lita** might not enjoy much in common with Gazza or Bryan Robson in terms of on-field achivements, but something they do share is the fact they were all injured in bed-related incidents.

Lita was ruled out for the first month of the 2007/08 campaign after damaging a leg muscle – stretching in bed after waking up. "He woke up and stretched while in bed and he has done something to his leg," commented the then Royals manager Steve Coppell. "It is not an injury that should be ridiculed or made light of." Of course not.

The former England Under-21 player joined Middlesbrough in August 2009, a club also associated with Gascoigne and Robson.

Leroy Lita, safer standing up

No.30

Lucozade –
A bleach
alternative

Lucozade

BETTER THAN LUCOZADE?

PAT HOLLAND, WEST HAM UNITED
Venue: Team bath

THE story goes that in 1978 following a game for the Hammers, the midfielder relaxed in the team bath by enjoying a swig of what he assumed to be a certain fizzy drink often associated with sport – or hospital visits. Said beverage actually turned out to be bleach. Latterly coach at MK Dons, Holland was rushed to hospital to have his stomach pumped.

No.31

VIDEO GAMES, INTERNATIONAL

DAVID JAMES, LIVERPOOL & ENGLAND
Venue: Various

ROBERT GREEN, ENGLAND B
Venue: Madejski Stadium, Reading

AT over 6ft 4ins tall, **David James** had all the physical attributes to become a top-class international goalkeeper. But in his early days, especially during his time as a Liverpool player, his mental capacity to deal with the expectations of the fans left a lot to be desired.

After a series of high-profile clangers, particularly in games against Manchester United, James' nadir came after a fixture at Middlesbrough when he revealed his darkest pleasure in life – the video game. He cited the habit for his lack of concentration during games, and he was apparently forced to miss a game due to RSI in his thumb caused by excessive video game usage.

David James collides with Martin Keown during England's friendly with Holland in 2001

Robert Green hides his embarrassment after being carried off injured

Four years later, James had reformed his career following spells at Aston Villa and West Ham United. But even then, he was prone to the odd gaffe – highlighted when he played for England against Holland in an international friendly match.

Trailing 2-0 with the Dutch running riot at White Hart Lane, England made seven substitutions at half-time. Barely a minute into the second period, they were forced to change another two when James and Martin Keown were forced off injured, after comically colliding when Jimmy-Floyd Hasselbaink went close to making the score 3-0.

The curse of the England substitute goalkeeper struck again prior to the 2006 World Cup, when West Ham's **Robert Green** ruptured his groin while taking a goal-kick during a 'B' international against Belarus. The visitors promptly scored from the botched kick. The injury forced Green to miss the tournament in Germany, as well as the start of the 2006/07 season with his club.

119

Gaming in the 21st century – David James uninterested

No.32

HORSEPLAY

MAURICE JOHNSTON, EVERTON
Venue: Formby, Merseyside

IT'S fair to assess the Scottish striker's spell at Everton as something of a mixed bag. There were some crucial goals, including strikes in Merseyside derby matches in successive seasons at Goodison Park. But there were also off-the-field scrapes, and a succession of injury problems. Matters took a turn for the farcical over Christmas 1992. Having apparently fallen down the stairs at his home, he somehow grappled with his daughter's rocking horse – and came off worse. A broken jaw was the diagnosis, and a month on the sidelines.

Blues boss Howard Kendall commented at the time: "He has a facial injury following an accident at home. I know what people are going to think. It was over the Christmas period. You are talking about someone with a facial injury and people are going to jump to conclusions."

Johnston also ended up with a black eye from the incident, and having cost Everton £1.5m when he signed from Rangers in 1991, he was released and joined Hearts less than two years later. He was most recently director of soccer at Toronto FC in Major League Soccer.

Maurice Johnston –
Safer on away turf?

121

Paddy Kenny bares the
scars of his night out

122

TWO SIDES OF THE STREET

PADDY KENNY, SHEFFIELD UNITED
Venue: Halifax, Yorkshire

ROBERT HUGHES, SUTTON UNITED
Venue: Crete, Greece

WARNED by his then club manager Neil Warnock to keep a low profile, Blades stopper **Paddy Kenny** apparently ignored the advice, going for a night out in his home town of Halifax in 2006. Unfortunately, he became involved in an altercation with a former friend outside a curry house, related to a domestic matter. He subsequently had his eyebrow bitten off, requiring 12 stitches. He might have been partial to a spot of Yorkshire grappling, but antics like this can result in long-term hospitalisation.

In the summer of 2008, former Oxford United player **Robert Hughes** was attacked by five youths outside a nightclub on holiday in Crete, and left in a coma. Greek doctors said he was 48 hours from death and warned he would be paralysed.

When Hughes finally awoke after two weeks' intensive care, he suffered complete amnesia and to this day is unable to recall anything from the last 10 years apart from his love for football. He cannot remember playing for Oxford United at all. His injuries meant he had to miss the whole of the 2008/09 season.

The player, from Croydon, south London, had to relearn everything – even how to eat and move. His mother Maggie Hughes said: "We went back to the simple things in life. We did things like putting gum in his mouth to help him chew, lifting his arms and moving his fingers to make him use them. It took time but eventually we got him to do it himself."

Mrs Hughes had no doubt that football brought him back from the brink. She heard a commotion by her son's bed and ran to see what was happening. Her son was still in a coma, kicking an imaginary football. "I could not believe it," she said. "I stayed there for weeks praying for him to move, and when he does it is a football manoeuvre. From that moment on I knew he was going to make it."

Robert then defied expectations by learning to walk, and he is remarkably playing football once more. He played a part in Welling United's 3-2 friendly defeat to Millwall in the summer of 2009, and impressed sufficiently to be offered a contract by the Conference South team.

Curry and Paddy Kenny – Far from an ideal match

No.34

GOOD MOVEMENT?

KAYODE KESHIRO, NIGERIA UNDER-17S
Venue: Hotel in Bauchi, Nigeria

THE forward was a big prospect in his country, being included in the squad for the 1989 World Youth Championships in Scotland. The tournament was still three months away, with the players living at a hotel back in Nigeria. On the eve of a friendly, it is claimed he was walking along the hotel corridor, with a defensive team-mate going in the opposite direction. When they met, the defender is said to have made a mock move as if to dispossess Keshiro of an imaginary ball. He reacted instinctively, with a feint as if carrying the ball around his opponent. Unfortunately, the whole incident ended up causing a thigh problem for the striker, who missed the friendly.

Alex Kolinko (right) keeps a mysteriously low profile in the Crystal Palace dugout

No.35

SUPER SUBS?

ALEX KOLINKO, CRYSTAL PALACE
Venue: Selhurst Park, London

BARRY FERGUSON & ALLAN MCGREGOR, SCOTLAND
Venue: Hampden Park, Glasgow

BRETT SOLKHON, CORBY TOWN
Venue: Rockingham Triangle

127

LATVIAN **Alex Kolinko** made a big impression on his Crystal Palace manager Trevor Francis – unfortunately for all the wrong reasons. The goalkeeper was hit around the head by his boss in August 2002, Francis having taken offence when Kolinko – who was on the bench – allegedly laughed after the Eagles' opponents, Bradford City, had scored through Andy Tod. After the 1-1 draw, Kolinko claimed: "I was not laughing in the dugout. The manager punched me on the nose. I have not been given an explanation as to why he did it. My nose is very sore and bruised."

Misbehaving substitutes don't always experience injuries as a result of their tomfoolery. Others do.

In 2009, Rangers pair **Barry Ferguson** and **Allan McGregor** were banned from playing for Scotland indefinitely after they were filmed making rude hand gestures at TV cameras while waiting on the substitutes' bench.

The duo had been left out of Scotland's starting line-up for the World Cup qualifier against Iceland in April 2009, this following a late-night drinking session after a defeat in Holland only days before – something that was widely reported in the Scottish press. The emergence of the players' gestures during the Iceland match at Hampden Park – and the public reaction to it – forced drastic action to be taken.

Both players issued an apology for their actions and spoke of their disappointment that their international careers were over. Ferguson said: "I deeply regret what happened and the events during the last week, and apologise wholeheartedly for the embarrassment caused to Scotland, Rangers, both sets of supporters and my friends and family.

"I have always considered playing for Rangers and Scotland an honour and a privilege and nothing will change that. I am bitterly disappointed by the announcement that I will not be selected for Scotland again."

In non-league football, Corby Town midfielder **Brett Solkhon** was injured warming up on the sidelines after stretching too far for a misplaced pass, which had gone out of play. It ruled him out for one week of pre-season training in 2009.

Alex Kolinko and (inset) Andy Tod – The man to blame

129

Barry Ferguson (above)
and Allan McGregor
play predict the score –
possibly...

No.36

PRIVATE PARTS

KEVIN KYLE, SUNDERLAND
Venue: Kyle household

KIERAN DURKAN, ROCHDALE
Venue: Unknown

DEAN BARRICK, PRESTON NORTH END
Venue: Unknown

KEVIN KYLE suffered the ignominy of scalding his testicles in April 2006 after his then eight-month-old baby son – who he had been preparing to feed – knocked a jug of boiling water into his father's lap.

The giant Scottish striker can sleep safe in the knowledge that he isn't the only player to have blistered his balls.

Some time in the late 1990s, Rochdale winger **Kieran Durkan** suffered the same injury, only on this occasion it was sustained thanks to a clumsy team-mate. Dale centre-back Richard Green accidentally spilt the contents of a boiling kettle onto Durkan's lap, with much of the water spraying painfully over his particulars. Luckily, neither of these injuries endured any lasting affect.

Each year, more than 112,000 people in this country enter emergency rooms with scald burns. Scalding is caused by spills, immersion, or other contact with hot water, food and hot beverages or steam.

Kyle, meanwhile, now captains Kilmarnock in Scotland, while Durkan recently spent time in the League of Wales with Caernarfon.

There is also the case of **Dean Barrick**, who in 1997 was ruled out for a month after supposedly spilling the contents of a coffee pot onto a sensitive area.

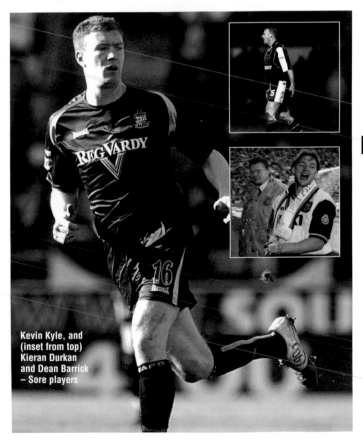

Kevin Kyle, and (inset from top) Kieran Durkan and Dean Barrick – Sore players

131

No.37

BOARD GAMES

LIONEL LETIZI, PARIS SAINT GERMAIN
Venue: Unknown

WHILE playing Scrabble in December 2002, the French goalkeeper strained back muscles trying to pick up a piece from the floor – the identity of which was never revealed. Consequently he missed two games – a 1-0 defeat to Rennes, and a 1-1 draw against Bordeaux. Letizi later confirmed to his club's website: "I completely put my back out."

Apparently more than 80% of injuries in the work place are sustained to the back – hardly an excuse for Letizi.

No.**38**

FRIENDLY FIRE?

JARI LITMANEN, FULHAM
Venue: Various

FRED HARRISON, MIDDLESBROUGH FAN
Venue: Riverside Stadium, Middlesbrough

IGOR, FORTALEZA
Venue: Brazil

THE Cottagers' reserve goalkeeper Ricardo Batista –
presumably accidentally – ended the brief Fulham career of
veteran playmaker Jari Litmanen in April 2008. The player fired
a ball which struck the back of the Finland international's head
from close range, ruling him out of the Premier League game
against Manchester City. His boss, Roy Hodgson also revealed
that the player had once been hit in the eye by a ring-pull from
a drinks can, opened by a club colleague in Sweden.

During his two spells in England with Liverpool and then the
Craven Cottage side, Litmanen was unlucky with injuries. At
Anfield, he missed out on the club's cup treble of FA, League

Jari Litmanen, in more control of this football

134

A Middlesbrough fan – Presumably not a grandfather of six

and UEFA Cups in 2001 with a long-term hand injury. Despite being revered by fans, he was allowed to leave for Ajax and after spells back in Finland, Germany and Sweden, he returned to the Premier League in early 2008 at Craven Cottage.

Despite being a long time favourite of manager Hodgson (he managed the Finnish national team and tried to sign him as a 17-year-old while in charge of Malmo), Litmanen didn't feature in a single game for the west Londoners because of fears about his general health. This, in the wake of being hit on the back of the head with the ball.

In the same season (2007/08), it was reported that a stray shot also injured Middlesbrough supporter **Fred Harrison**. The grandfather of six suffered a broken wrist when he tried to stop a shot from Manchester United's Cristiano Ronaldo in their April encounter at the Riverside Stadium.

"As soon as it left Ronaldo's foot, I could see where it was going," he told local media. "I had my glasses on, so I automatically put my hands up. It was a great save which probably Mark Schwarzer couldn't even match, but it was hit so hard it broke my wrist.

"When it hit me I said: 'That was a good one'. The ball was travelling at an unbelievable speed. I only just got my arm up in time, otherwise I would probably have been knocked out."

He only found out a few days later when his wrist swelled up. A spokesman for United said: "Cristiano would be very sorry about his broken wrist if he knew about it."

Another widely noted injury caused in similar 'kicking' circumstances was suffered by Brazilian midfielder **Igor**. Playing against Sao Caetano, he felt the full force of a team-mate's kick. Presumably the work of a training ground routine gone wrong, the player attempted to run up to dummy or run over the ball at a free-kick – at the same time as his team-mate, Bechara, who was swinging his right leg to take a shot at goal. The latter ended up hitting and breaking the leg of the former.

No.39

Steve Lomas (left) and Joe Ledley – Holiday nightmares?

RELAXING BREAK

STEVE LOMAS, WEST HAM UNITED
Venue: Disneyland, California, USA

JOE LEDLEY, CARDIFF CITY
Venue: Paris, France

RECOVERING from a shin problem in summer 2002, it would be assumed that Hammers' skipper **Steve Lomas** could look forward to resting his weary limbs. Unfortunately, the midfielder managed to aggravate the problem. The cause? "I was doing a lot of walking in Disneyland."

Another to suffer the holiday blues was Wales midfielder **Joe Ledley**, who was forced to don protective strapping in a World Cup qualifier with Russia in September 2009. He broke a bone in his hand – slipping on steps while on a mini-break in France.

No.40

137

BRUSH STROKES

ALAN MULLERY, ENGLAND
Venue: Unknown

THE Spurs midfielder, who had yet to be capped by his country, missed England's tour to South America in 1964 after putting his back out brushing his teeth.

Mullery may have been capped earlier had he followed the lead of *Carry On* actor Kenneth Williams. In letters from the comedian planned to be auctioned off in 2008, he complained: 'Life is so hard. First thing in the morning there's the teeth. That means toothpaste. That's got to be squeezed out. It's all work.'

Gary Naysmith –
On safe ground?

No.41

I WANTED THE GROUND TO SWALLOW ME UP

GARY NAYSMITH, SCOTLAND UNDER-21S
Venue: Bosnia

IAN WRIGHT, ARSENAL
Venue: Highbury, London

FERNANDO HIERRO, REAL MADRID
Venue: Unknown

WHILE at Hearts, full-back **Gary Naysmith** suffered the unfortunate fate of falling down a manhole during a match against Bosnia & Herzegovina in the late 1990s. Skippering the Under-21 side, the Scot apparently recalled the incident thus: "I was taking a long throw when I stood on the drain cover and it disappeared under my feet. You don't expect it to happen in international football."

It was not an isolated football incident. In February 1993, **Ian Wright** missed England's World Cup qualifier with San Marino after damaging his groin. Aiming to complete a hat-trick for Arsenal in a 2-0 FA Cup victory over Nottingham Forest, Wright challenged the goalkeeper, and in doing so his studs went from underneath him, "probably caught in a pot hole", according to his manager George Graham. Wright had yet to score for England, and he missed out on an ideal opportunity to break his duck – even Carlton Palmer was on target in a 6-0 win days later. Wright would score four in the return, although the 7-1 win was not enough to earn England a place at the 1994 World Cup.

Wright would also suffer another injury in England's cause during the 1998 World Cup – although he was in his home gym at the time. Exercising on weights, he leapt up in excitement after seeing Michael Owen equalise against Romania – twisting his ankle in the process.

Real Madrid captain **Fernando Hierro**, who would enjoy a season in England with Bolton Wanderers at the end of his playing career, also suffered a non-football playing injury at the start of the 1997/98 campaign. It was claimed that he put his foot through a manhole cover, having been trying to escape paparazzi at the time.

In 'civilian' life, one 15-year-old girl in the USA suffered the same fate, failing to notice an uncovered manhole due to her attention being taken by a mobile phone.

Ian Wright pre-fall, and
(inset) Fernando Hierro

No.42

Norbert Nigbur (second right) – restaurant woe

LEAVE A TIP

NORBERT NIGBUR, SCHALKE 04
Venue: Restaurant in West Germany

THE West German international goalkeeper's career was all but ended in 1980 after he tore the meniscus cartilage in his knee, locking it in the process. The cause? Standing up – this when leaving the table at the end of a meal in a restaurant, while out with his fiancée. The incident came in April, just weeks before the European Championships, where he was expected to be first choice. He required immediate surgery, and never added to his six West Germany caps.

No.43

BUZZING

ANACLET ODHIAMBO, ABINGDON UNITED
Venue: AlderSmith Stadium, Frome

AN hour into Abingdon's opening-day match at Frome in the Zamaretto League Division One South & West in August 2009, the visitors find themselves 3-0 down. Matters take a turn for the worse when Anaclet Odhiambo gets stung by a wasp – the striker later citing the club's new bright yellow home shirt as a factor. "It's a little bit too yellow. If the sun goes down a bit and there aren't as many bugs about we'll be alright. I've been to the doctors to get some cream."

Having left the field of play, he returned to the pitch and almost immediately set up team-mate Luke Holden, who raced through…and hit the side netting with his effort. Manager Andy Slater later commented: "I have to admit that Anaclet moved very quickly after the moment he was stung." There was no, erm, sting in the tale for Frome though, who ran out 3-1 winners.

Do I not like yellow:
Would a wasp be
attracted to this lot?

No.44

BRING ON THE WALL

MARTIN PALERMO, VILLARREAL
Venue: Ciudad de Valencia, Valencia

THE Argentina international striker, having netted against Levante in the Copa del Rey in November 2001, rushed over to a group of fans to celebrate. Unfortunately, his jubilation was cut short when a pitch-side wall collapsed on him, breaking his tibia and fibula. He was out for six months and unfortunately, was forced to miss the following year's World Cup.

No.45

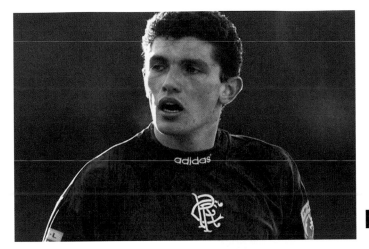

ONCE BITTEN

GORDAN PETRIC, RANGERS
Venue: Hampden Park, Glasgow

THE Serbian defender had settled well at Ibrox in his first season after moving from Dundee United in the summer of 1995. Unfortunately, his campaign would end after helping his side to victory over Celtic in the Scottish Cup semi-final. His goalkeeper, a certain Andy Goram, had bitten Petric on the elbow after he had come to collect a cross during the match. Days later, the wound had become poisonous and he was ordered by doctors to miss the final weeks of the season.

No.46

BRING YOUR KEEPER...TO THE SLAUGHTER

MART POOM, DERBY COUNTY
Venue: Tallinn, Estonia

THE Estonia goalkeeper was forced to miss a pre-season game with the Rams in July 2000 after picking up an injury – against an Iron Maiden XI. The band were in the city ahead of a concert, and a match was arranged to raise money for under-privileged children. Appearing as a guest player for his former club, Poom had gone upfield for a corner with his Flora Tallinn side 8-0 up. Unfortunately, he suffered concussion and a broken cheekbone following a collision with the opposition goalkeeper – although some reports also suggest the injury was actually to his genitals.

Mart Poom out of harm's way – in goal

No.47

SIN BIN

LUCAS RADEBE, LEEDS UNITED
Venue: Radebe driveway

THE injury-jinxed South African defender aggravated a knee injury in February 2003 when he fell on ice – taking the bins out at home. Coming in a season which saw Leeds struggling to survive in the top flight and who were already without a clutch of defenders due to injury, it wasn't the best of times to be losing another player. Manager Terry Venables reflected at the time: "It's not funny really. It's amazing what's going on."

No. 48

ON DOCTORS' ORDERS

RAMALHO
Venue: Unknown

MARCO BORRIELLO, AC MILAN
Venue: Private

BRAZILIAN forward **Ramalho** was apparently bed-ridden with a stomach upset for three days after swallowing a suppository intended to treat a dental infection. Why a suppository was used is anyone's guess – or even swallowed, but never mind.

A treatment of sorts was also blamed for a positive drugs test by Italian international striker **Marco Borriello** in late 2006. According to his girlfriend, the problem stemmed from a cream he used to treat an infection in a sensitive area – which had been caught from her.

No.49

TERMINAL TROUBLE

MILAN RAPAIC, HADJUK SPLIT
Venue: Airport

THE Croatian was forced to miss the start of the 1995/96 season – after sticking his boarding pass in his eye at the airport. Then only 21, the midfielder/forward was presumably a little too keen to see if he had a window seat, and subsequently caused an eye injury.

No.50

SLIP-ONS AN ALTERNATIVE

MICHAEL RENSING, BAYERN MUNICH
Venue: Unknown

THE goalkeeper injured his back ahead of a UEFA Cup round of 32 tie with Aberdeen in February 2008 – bending to tie his shoelaces. "Michael hurt his back while tying his shoes…in an emergency we'll find someone to tie his laces for him," coach Ottmar Hitzfeld remarked.

He's not the only sportsperson to pick up an injury in this way – wicketkeeper Nick Wilton apparently missed a second XI match for Sussex in 2000 having suffered a similar strain.

The Micah Richards mask, now available at all good sports retailers

No.51

BEING ILL – IT'S A SWINE

MICAH RICHARDS, MANCHESTER CITY
Venue: Ayia Napa, Cyprus

GRAHAM KAVANAGH, CARLISLE UNITED
Venue: Unknown

BRITISH BEACH TEAM
Venue: Not Austria

RUSSIA FANS
Venue: Not Wales

153

THE year 2009 will be known as the time that swine flu entered public consciousness. It affected everyone – including footballers. Micah Richards was one of the first, and arguably the most high-profile casualty. The England defender was stranded in a hotel room in Cyprus for a week, after contracting the virus while on holiday in July. He was not allowed to travel back to the UK until fully recovered, although he could see the funny side later on. "I'll get some stick from the lads when I do return – they will probably all turn up to training in surgical masks."

Graham Kavanagh, the former Republic of Ireland international, was one of the first to be diagnosed. "After three or four days of pre-season, I started feeling really tired," the veteran midfielder said. "At that point, I thought, 'This is the way it must feel when your legs start to go.' So I was delighted when it just turned out to be swine flu!"

The **British beach football team** were apparently kicked out of the Nations Cup in Austria due to the swine flu risk they posed. The team were favourites to win the event in Linz, northern Austria, but organisers said that they would not be able to take part as there was too much of a risk that the British side could contaminate other teams.

Organisers of the international beach soccer event said the disease was clearly an epidemic in Britain while Austria had seen less than 100 infections at that stage. However, this was denied by a spokesman for the team, stating that the players simply couldn't afford to make the trip.

Before their World Cup qualifier against Wales in September, **Russia fans** were warned not to travel to avoid contracting the disease. Excitable fans indulging in "intense shouting" could encourage the spread of the virus, a spokesman for the Russian FA warned. The Russian supporters' association responded by jokingly advising fans to drink copious amounts of Welsh whisky to prevent symptoms taking hold in Cardiff.

In the same month, experts with the French and Swedish national associations had proferred advice related to avoiding the transmission of swine flu. The French suggested players cut down on goal celebrations, while the Swedes wanted to avoid shaking hands at the start and end of matches.

Graham Kavanagh, still going strong and (inset) Matt Le Tissier and Neil Pointon – beach boys

Welsh fans – More welcome in Russia

Welsh whisky – Flu deterrent

155

Peter Schmeichel pays
for his outfield lunge,
and (inset) Joe Lewis –
England forward

No.52

THERE'S A REASON YOU'RE IN GOAL

PETER SCHMEICHEL, MANCHESTER UNITED
Venue: Old Trafford, Manchester

157

DANISH keeper Peter Schmeichel pulled a hamstring attempting to tackle Dennis Bergkamp in March 1998. Not only was the United No. 1 way out of his goal – he was actually in Arsenal's half when he attempted to make the challenge having ventured upfield in a forlorn search for an equaliser. That said, Schmeichel did net for United in a UEFA Cup tie in 1996, scoring a total of 13 goals during his career.

There have been numerous occasions when goalkeepers have gone up the other end of the pitch to score crucial goals, although one goalkeeper actually came on as an outfield player in the summer of 2009. Peterborough United's Joe Lewis acted as an emergency forward for England Under-21s after boss Stuart Pearce ran out of options in a friendly against their Azerbaijan counterparts. "Joe thought he ran around more than Fraizer Campbell but we'll look back at the video to see," Pearce commented after the 7-0 stroll.

No.53

CATCH OF THE DAY

DAVID SEAMAN, ARSENAL
Venues: Various

THREE separate incidents mark the one-time England keeper as somebody susceptible to injury. Having just joined Arsenal from QPR, he was named as third choice goalkeeper for England's 1990 World Cup campaign – although he would eventually have to step down from second reserve duties. He suffered a broken finger in training after former club team-mate Paul Parker had blasted a ball, which was off the pitch. It struck Seaman on the hand as he was waiting for a corner to be delivered on the pitch – thus facing the other way to where Parker had delivered the 'shot'. The impact bent his hand back – and caused the problem.

Seaman also damaged knee ligaments in the mid-90s, another footballer to suffer the curse of the TV remote control. He was bending down to pick it up when he did the damage.

Further misfortunate befell the Yorkshireman when, already out with a knee injury, he went carp fishing and put his shoulder out while reeling in a 26-pounder. A persistent shoulder problem would eventually end his playing career.

David Seaman –
Injury free?

159

Tommy Smith –
Second-best to
a pick-axe

160

No.54

YOU SHOULD HAVE SEEN THE PICK-AXE

TOMMY SMITH, LIVERPOOL
Venue: The Smith garden

AS noted earlier, the 'Anfield Iron' missed the 1978 European Cup final due to a gardening accident with a pick-axe. He had decided to carry on for one more season having delayed his retirement at the end of the 1976/77 season, but a fairytale ending proved elusive after the accident, which caused a broken bone in his right foot. He would go on to play one more season in Wales, helping Swansea City, managed by old Liverpool team-mate John Toshack, win promotion from the old Third Division.

No.55

IRON MAN

MICHAEL STENSGAARD, LIVERPOOL
Venue: Unknown

THE Danish goalkeeper was a hot prospect when he joined the Reds in 1994 from Hvidovre IF in his homeland. Unfortunately, he would never play a first-team game for Liverpool, being forced to quit top-level football after dislocating a shoulder – erecting an ironing board, just a year after signing. He would later recover to play in his homeland, retiring in 2001.

Michael Stensgaard –
Creases remain

163

No.56

IMPRESSIVE FEET

BOB TAYLOR, WEST BROMWICH ALBION
Venue: Various

SIR BOBBY ROBSON, ENGLAND
Venue: Mexico

BAGGIES legend **Bob Taylor** injured his Achilles in 2002 as a result of friction from his new leather shoes. He would be ruled out of action for two months.

The late **Sir Bobby Robson** was another person that suffered from dodgy footwear. In the 1986 World Cup held in Mexico, Robson forgot his boots for a training session being held more than half-an-hour away from the team hotel.

Luckily future England boss Glenn Hoddle had a spare brand new and sharing the same shoe size as Robson, he offered them to his manager. After the session had finished, Robson threw them back at Hoddle complaining of terrible cramps. "There's no way they're a size 9," the befuddled coach exclaimed.

Hoddle examined the boots and found that Robson had failed to remove the safety mesh paper that accompanies all new boots. Robson promptly missed the following day's training with blisters.

Glenn Hoddle –
Size 9?

168

No.57

UP TO HIS NECK

JACK TAYLOR, EVERTON
Venue: Old Trafford, Manchester

ONE of only six players to make over 400 league appearances for Everton, the Scottish defender played in three FA Cup finals for the Toffees, being victorious in 1906. But the competition would end up seeing the end for the player as a professional. Playing in the semi-final replay against Barnsley in 1910, Taylor was struck by a fierce shot in the throat, damaging his larynx. The following day's *Liverpool Echo* reported the incident thus:

'A kick in the neck caused him intense pain. White approached his clubmate, but Taylor was in agony and could not get his breath. Not until two spectators (apparently medical men) lent their aid did Taylor find any ease. Drs Whitford and Baxter attended to the unfortunate player when he was taken to the dressing room and it was discovered that the larynx of the throat had been damaged, if not fractured.'

Taylor refused to leave the pitch for long, despite the seriousness of the injury in a game which would see Everton lose 3-0 – in an era well before substitutes could be introduced. They were also effectively down to nine men when goalkeeper Billy Scott tore the webbing between the second and third fingers of his hand.

It would prove his 456th and final game for the club. He would end his career at local amateur side South Liverpool.

No.58

A RIGHT SHOWER

CARLOS TEVEZ, MANCHESTER CITY
LEE HODGES, BARNET
THOMAS MYHRE, EVERTON
Venues: Various washing facilities

CARLOS TEVEZ'S career at Manchester City did not get off to the most auspicious of starts when he suffered a bizarre injury before he'd even played for the club. Tevez apparently lost his balance trying to get out of the shower in August 2009, aggravating a heel problem in the process.

Considering City's exorbitant spending in 2008 and 2009, it is surprising they didn't recommend a player reportedly on £150,000 a week to buy a non-slip bath mat.

The Argentinian, however, isn't the first player to fall victim of a soapy foot in the shower. In 1996, **Lee Hodges** of Barnet wrenched his groin when he leant over the shower door to grab a towel. He missed more than a month of the season.

In 1999 Thomas Myhre, then of Everton, lost his footing in the bath and broke his ankle – an injury that eventually led to him losing his place in the team and being sold.

Such injuries, though, are nothing compared to what Tevez suffered as a child when he accidentally scalded his neck with boiling water, causing him third degree burns and keeping him hospitalised in intensive care for nearly two months. It left him with a distinctive scar that runs from his right ear to chest.

Upon later joining Boca Juniors, Tevez refused an offer from the club to have them cosmetically improved, saying the scars were a part of who he was in the past and who he is in the present.

According to 2008 statistics, children are most at danger in the shower with 15 people daily in the UK reporting injuries.

Lee Hodges (right) attempts to keep his balance

Thomas Myhre – May stick to the bath

No.59

TRADING BLOWS

LEE THORPE, ROCHDALE
Venue: Team coach

KEITH O'NEILL, COVENTRY CITY
Venue: Fairground

MUCH-TRAVELLED frontman **Lee Thorpe**, already facing a spell on the sidelines in May 2008, extended his period out of the game – after shattering his arm in an arm-wrestling incident on the team bus.

Travelling with the squad to their League Two play-off semi-final, first-leg match at Darlington, Thorpe was already ruled out due to a dead leg. Thorpe and team-mate Rene Howe (who played in the match) passed the time with an arm wrestle – with painful consequences. Striker Chris Dagnall later revealed: "Everyone on the bus heard the snap, it was that loud. He's got Rene to blame for that."

Arm-wrestling has been enjoyed by people over many hundreds of years. Like with any male ego contest, there is a degree of danger. According to specialists, it places enormous torque/twist on the upper arm's humerus bone to a degree seen in few other physical activities. Most people's bones are not accustomed to being significantly stressed in this direction, and injuries can occur surprisingly easily. The arm typically fails because of a diagonal break at or below the mid-point between the shoulder and the elbow. Obviously this wasn't at the forefront of Thorpe's mind when he travelled to the north-east.

Republic of Ireland winger **Keith O'Neill's** career was ravaged by injury problems related to the condition spondylosis, a degenerative arthratic condition which affects the joints around the lower back. However, sometimes the injuries weren't always the fault of his failing body. After being close to another comeback, this time from a double leg fracture, he broke his hand in November 2002. The break was actually caused on a fairground punchbag, O'Neill having been invited to test his strength at a charity event.

Lee Thorpe, next time he may stick to cards, and (inset) Keith O'Neill: Punchbag woe

MMC
estates

No.60

WEMBLEY BREAKS

BERT TRAUTMANN, MANCHESTER CITY
GERRY BYRNE, LIVERPOOL
RAY WOOD, MANCHESTER UNITED
ROY DWIGHT, NOTTINGHAM FOREST
DAVE WHELAN, BLACKBURN ROVERS
Venue: Wembley Stadium, London

ONE of the most famous injuries in the history of the game in England involved **Bert Trautmann**, the German goalkeeper who broke his neck with 17 minutes still to play during the 1956 FA Cup final against Birmingham City. Diving at the feet of Peter Murphy, Trautmann suffered serious injury but he played on, making crucial saves to preserve City's 3-1 advantage. His neck was noticeably crooked when he collected his medal, and an X-ray diagnosed the problem three days after the match.

The gallantry performed by Trautmann will surely never be repeated. But at the time, he wasn't alone in presenting such fortitude in an effort to help his team.

In the 1965 FA Cup final, Liverpool left-back **Gerry Byrne** played a full 90 minutes and extra time with a broken collarbone after a late challenge from Leeds United captain Bobby Collins – the incident had happened in only the third minute. With no substitutes permitted, Byrne had no option but to keep on playing.

He and his team-mates, not to mention Bill Shankly and his coaching team on the Liverpool bench, somehow managed to keep the extent of Byrne's injury a secret from the Leeds players and staff. Byrne even managed to set up Roger Hunt's opening goal at the beginning of extra time, before Billy Bremner equalised for Leeds.

Liverpool were not to be denied as Ian St John headed home the winner late on during the second period, earning the Reds their first ever FA Cup. Shankly spoke highly of Byrne in an interview after the final, saying: "It was a performance of raw courage from the boy."

Gerry Byrne (back row, right) lines up with his Liverpool team-mates

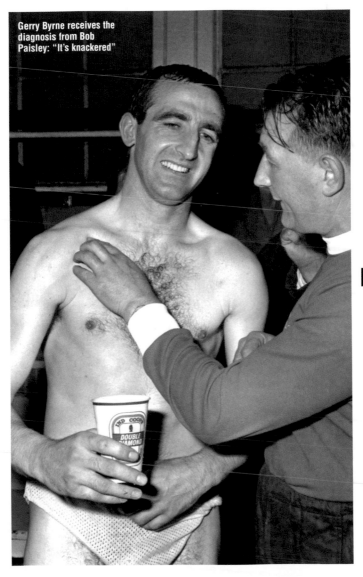

Gerry Byrne receives the diagnosis from Bob Paisley: "It's knackered"

180

An injured Ray Wood (right) leaves the field alongside Aston Villa's Peter McParland. It was the forward's shoulder charge that injured Wood

Roy Dwight recovers in hospital from his broken leg, while (below) Dave Whelan is stretchered off

181

Trautmann and Byrne's injuries led to calls for the FA to allow a sub to be selected by each team in competitive matches. Manchester United goalkeeper **Ray Wood** (1957 final) had played on as an outfield player, and then back in goal after suffering a broken cheekbone and a loss of consciousness in a collision, and in two successive FA Cup finals (1959 and 1960), **Roy Dwight** and Dave Whelan were carried off with broken legs.

By 1967, the FA finally relented and from then on, the first substitutes were allowed in the final.

182

No.61

STEAMING IN

TOMMY TYNAN, TORQUAY UNITED
Venue: Gloucestershire

THE striker was first given his chance in football by Bill Shankly, after winning a talent contest organised by the *Liverpool Echo* in the early 1970s – the prize being an apprenticeship at Liverpool. He went on to enjoy a decent career in the lower divisions, remaining a Plymouth Argyle legend where he scored well over 100 goals.

In the veteran phase of his playing career, he was dismissed by Torquay United in June 1991 after being involved in a bust-up with his skipper Wes Saunders. Relaxing in a country club ahead of the team's successful Fourth Division play-off final victory over Blackpool the previous month, the duo apparently scuffled, with Tynan suffering a cut above his right eye. A couple of hours later, Tynan visited Saunders' room and picked up the nearest object available – in this case a kettle – and hit the player with it, leaving him with cuts and bruises.

No.62

LIKE SNOW OFF A SHOVEL

IMRE VARADI, LEEDS UNITED
Venue: Neighbour's drive

184 PEOPLE associate snow sports with sustaining injuries that can ruin a holiday, especially those who are beginners or novices. But Imre Varadi, who played for 16 professional clubs in England, wasn't on the piste when he pulled his back whilst at Leeds United in the early 1990s – he was shovelling snow in his neighbour's drive.

In 2001, Bolivian footballers risked potential injury (or worse) when they played a game in the snow at the highest ever recorded altitude on Mount Sajama, South America's second tallest mountain. Two of the players who were due to take part did not even make it on to the pitch and were struck down with sickness as they climbed their way to the 6542m (21,424ft) summit.

In 2009, hospitals around the UK reported an increase in the number of injuries from falls because of snow. The Department of Health said all the public services were under pressure and the NHS was working extremely hard to minimise the impact on patients. It reported that during times of heavy snowfall, hospitals received 10% more phone calls than usual.

No.63

HOLE IN THE FOOT

DARIUS VASSELL, ASTON VILLA
Venue: Unknown

FRANK TALIA, WYCOMBE WANDERERS
Venue: The Talia Garden

ONE-TIME England frontman **Darius Vassell** famously picked up a toe infection in autumn 2002 after trying to burst a blood blister trapped under his toe nail – with a power drill. Half his nail went in the process.

It appears Vassell was one of the luckier injury victims. At the beginning of the 21st century, a 62-year-old man in America committed suicide by drilling through his anterior chest wall with an electric power drill. In 2008, a woman in Australia accidentally drilled through her cervical spine – but recovered to tell the tale.

Another player to suffer angst from an electrical item is **Frank Talia**, an Australian goalkeeper formerly with Blackburn Rovers and Swindon Town. He missed the start of the 2004/05 season with Wycombe Wanderers after slicing off a toe when he fell over while mowing his lawn. Despite missing a digit, he soon returned to the squad before retiring in 2007.

A similar fate also befell Arsenal legend Charlie George in retirement – although he lost a finger on his right hand.

189

Frank Talia – Lawn woes

No.64

SLIDE RULE

PATRICK VIEIRA, ARSENAL
Venue: Highbury, North London

After scoring the second goal in the Gunners' 3-2 defeat of Manchester United in November 1997, the midfielder celebrated by finishing with a lengthy sprint before sliding on his knees. The manoeuvre would force the French midfielder to be taken off at half-time, and he was ruled out for five weeks. However, he would come back in time to help the club to their second league and cup double.

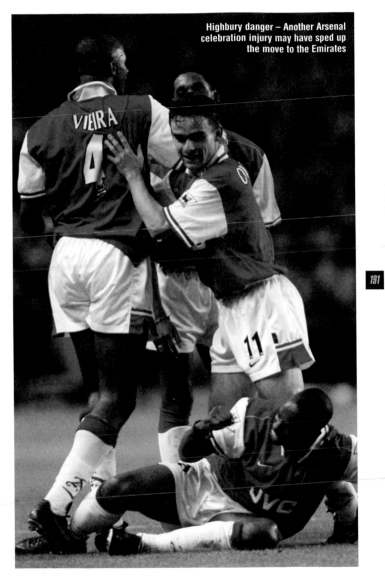

Highbury danger – Another Arsenal celebration injury may have sped up the move to the Emirates

191

David Villa sporting his
Euro 2008 injury

192

No.65

POINTING THE FINGER

DAVID VILLA, SPAIN
Venue: Tivoli Neu Stadium, Innsbruck

MARK KENNEDY, LIVERPOOL
Venue: Melwood, West Derby, Liverpool

SPAIN striker **David Villa** injured his finger celebrating the first goal of his hat-trick during the 4-1 win over Russia during Euro 2008. He told the media: "I got my finger caught in Fernando's [Torres] shirt when we were celebrating the goal, and bent it back."

A similar fate befell **Mark Kennedy** while at Liverpool. Hoping to make his first start for the Reds in over two years in March 1998, the winger's hopes were dashed in a bizarre training ground accident. He tore a tendon in his finger after apparently catching a digit on Oyvind Leonhardsen's training bib in a 50-50 challenge. He commented: "I sometimes feel I must be jinxed here." He would leave for Wimbledon before the month was out.

No.66

194

MARBLE BREAK

SIMON WHALEY, PRESTON
Venue: Hotel in Spain

THE winger was forced to miss the rest of the 2006/07 season after suffering a toe injury on a club break. The cause? A marble table top falling on his foot. "Simon got up in the night to go to the toilet and walked into a coffee table. The marble fell off and landed on his big toe," revealed Lilywhites manager Paul Simpson.

No.67

KEEPING BLOWS

CHRIS WOODS, ENGLAND
Venue: Unknown

ALEX STEPNEY, MANCHESTER UNITED
Venue: St Andrew's, Birmingham

NERY PUMPIDO, ARGENTINA
Venue: Unknown

VOLKAN DEMIREL, FENERBAHCE
Venue: Istanbul, Turkey

BRYAN KING, MILLWALL
Venue: Unknown

CHRIS WOODS was due to deputise for No. 1 Peter Shilton in an England friendly against Saudi Arabia in November 1988. Unfortunately, Woods missed out because he cut his finger open – after wrestling with the string on his tracksuit bottoms with a penknife. The setback for Rangers goalkeeper Woods enabled another injury-jinxed keeper into the fold – David Seaman would make his international debut in a 1-1 draw.

Chris Woods –
More comfortable
in shorts

196

The innocuous nature of Woods' injury is only matched by the misfortune of **Alex Stepney** in August 1975.

Manchester United's former goalkeeper, who signed for the club in 1966 after only three months at Chelsea (they made a then healthy £5,000 profit), managed to dislocate his jaw while shouting at defenders during a game against Birmingham City. He went down holding his face with nobody around him a minute into the second half. He later revealed: "I just shouted for the ball, when my jaw clicked and left me in agony. It was ridiculous. The damage must have been done when [Blues striker] Bob Hatton flattened me very early in the game."

Defender Brian Greenhoff ended up taking over in goal and he even kept a clean sheet, as two goals from Sammy McIlroy secured a 2-0 win.

Alex Stepney –
Sometimes it's best
to say nothing

197

Nery Pumpido fails to protect a 'safer' goal

Other goalkeepers to have endured unusual injuries are Argentina's **Nery Pumpido**, Turkey's **Volkan Demirel** and **Bryan King** at Millwall.

Pumpido came close to losing a finger after catching his wedding ring on a rogue nail on the crossbar in 1985.

Demirel suffered a dislocated shoulder after falling over throwing his shirt into the Fenerbahce fans – he'd helped his club side to a 2-1 victory over arch-rivals Galatasaray.

And finally King received a six-inch wound to the face after being on the receiving end of a practical joke. Team-mate Billy Neil, sporting a sovereign ring, was meant to pull his punch – he ended up connecting with an eye socket.

Volkan Demirel –
Keeping his shirt to
himself, and (inset)
Bryan King

199

No.**68**

200

FRANK ON A HIGH

FRANK WORTHINGTON, HUDDERSFIELD TOWN
Venue: Various

FRANK WORTHINGTON'S move to Liverpool in the summer of 1972 fell through after he failed two medicals. The first time, his proposed £150,000 transfer from Huddersfield Town broke down owing to high blood pressure – apparently brought on by excessive sexual activity. Told to have a two-week break in Majorca by Reds boss Bill Shankly, he returned for his second medical – and failed again. He instead moved to Leicester City after spending four days in a Huddersfield hospital having further tests and treatment.

No.69

A LONG STRETCH

ALAN WRIGHT, ASTON VILLA
Venue: £50,000 Ferrari

ONCE the smallest player in the Premier League at 5ft 4ins, height proved a factor in a bizarre injury for the full-back. He once strained his right knee stretching to reach the accelerator pedal on his new £50,000 Ferrari. The Ferrari problem never went away, forcing Wright to give up the motor. "The accelerator's position meant my right leg was bent slightly and my knee was giving me grief," admitted the player.

No.70

WRIGHT IDEA, WRONG EXECUTION

RICHARD WRIGHT, EVERTON
Venues: Wright household and Stamford Bridge, London

ONCE regarded as a long-term successor to David Seaman for club and country, goalkeeper Richard Wright's career has failed to reach the heady heights once predicted ever since he decided to join Arsenal from Ipswich Town in 2001.

After making his debut against Derby County, he made a series of fumbles and then limped out of a Champions League match with Deportivo La Coruna, slipping to third choice behind youth goalkeeper Stuart Taylor as well as Seaman. He was then offloaded to Everton, where he twice injured himself in bizarre circumstances.

In the summer of 2003 he suffered a serious injury falling from his loft after putting cases back following his holidays – the date was Friday 13th.

The subsequent arrival of Nigel Martyn forced Wright down the pecking order at Goodison, but his big chance came when the veteran aggravated an ankle problem early in 2006 in an FA Cup fourth round tie against Chelsea – an injury that eventually forced Martyn to retire. Unfortunately, Wright wasn't able to take his opportunity. Warming up ahead of the Cup replay at Stamford Bridge, he collided with a sign in front of the goal advising 'football not to be played here', injuring his ankle. He was ruled out of the game – Everton going down 4-1 – and despite playing a handful of games before the 2005/06 season was out, his big chance had gone – particularly when Tim Howard was brought in as No. 1 in the summer of 2006. Wright was released the following year.

Away from football, in 2007 a woman in New Zealand also ignored a warning sign – this one was on the edge of a glacier-carved chasm, into which she fell and lacerated her legs. However, unlike Wright at Goodison Park, police were called and a helicopter was deployed to rescue the woman.

Richard Wright ponders the sense of warming up in a goalmouth

Other Sport Media publications

Fascinating analysis of a unique
relationship between the sides

Complete guide to the strips worn by
Everton Football Club

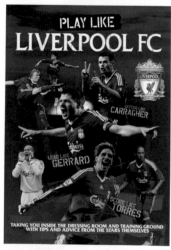

Advice and tips for budding footballers
from the Reds' first-team stars

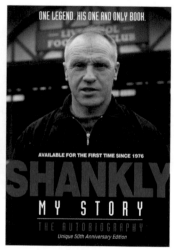

Re-release of the hard-hitting
autobiography, written in 1976

All of these titles, and more,
are available to order by calling 0845 143 0001,
or you can buy online at www.merseyshop.com

Other Sport Media publications

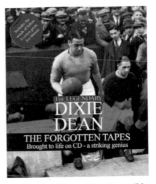

A celebration of the supporters' most memorable handiwork

The words of the great man on this CD, taken from 1977 interviews

Celebration of one of the greatest collections of football memorabilia

In-depth insight into the mind of a successful LFC talent spotter

All of these titles, and more, are available to order by calling 0845 143 0001, or you can buy online at www.merseyshop.com